Superficial Society

By
Maria Brusco Osso
and
Deanna Blackmon Jones

To Richie & Denise

'May God Bless
your going in &
Coming out in all
that You do!

I love You

Deanna Blackmon Jones

Acknowledgements and Dedication

To the glory of God

With love, we also dedicate this book to our
husbands and children

TABLE OF CONTENTS

PREFACE

How Did We Get Here?

Traditionally we have believed that our American society was shaped by our forefathers who beautifully crafted a government following Judeo-Christian values—a society that functions "under God." We now have a paradigm shift in thinking. This shift contradicts all perceived forms of authority as well as creating a perceived, "rational" order of society minus the oppressive biblical laws that supposedly hinder one's freedom and happiness. But what would this society look like without God—a superficial society without the principles or trappings of Christian ethics and morals?

Over the years, the paradigms of thought that reach beyond the Enlightenment period became refined with the hopes for the betterment of human understanding. For example, modernity in the nineteenth century rejected authority as a reaction to traditional beliefs. Postmodernism followed in the 1970's with its effort to neutralize trust in the individual, collective reasoning and the removal of as much semblance of Christianity from human affairs that could be accomplished. Little did anyone realize that in the background of the early 1920's, a group of German philosophers, psychologists and sociologists with an atheistic attitude established a think-tank referred to as the Frankfurt School in Frankfurt, Germany. Their goal was to develop an interdisciplinary social theory that would serve as the foundation for a post-Christian worldview. Contrary to modernity's framework of thought emphasizing individuality, the new social theory called, "Critical Theory," would focus on creating communities that would function without God.

Critical Theory has no limits in seeking to promote a free and self-determining type of society by dispelling ideological concepts. It eschews absolutism as well as all metaphysical and foundational theories. *Critical Theory* proposes concepts and concepts based on Western Marxism representative of the social and material world with the principles of equality and solidarity as its mainstay, usually denoted as "social justice."

The last quarter of the twentieth century saw both European and American societal traditional structures morph with the help of Critical Theory into a plethora of radical secular philosophies penetrating education, politics, social issues, the arts, and even theology. Without a doubt, the philosophy has contributed to the liberal, permissive and anti-Christian fabric of our lives.

Critical Theory's "New Thought" has been systematically creeping into all aspects of life jeopardizing our future as a society and as Christians. Unbeknownst to many, the pseudo-intellectuals have evolved beyond modernity and even post-modernism to a level that they believe constitutes a grasp on the true mechanisms of society. They are convinced that the key to change society lies in their hands. Intellectuals today revel at the lack of accuracy in traditional Christian para-digms as mass media tries to explain current events. While the most erudite people try to understand events from a tradi-tional Marxist perspective, these pseudo-intellectuals feel so superior that they laugh at all efforts of discovery. For they are not the typical; they have credence in an enlightened and progressive form of Marxism that has ignited the Western world with a new spirit to the detriment of all society.

"See to it that no one take you captive by philosophy and empty deceit, according to human tradition, according to elemental spirits of the world, and not according to Christ" (Col. 2:8).

Understand the Background to Our Current Crisis

Christians who want to think and speak intelligently about the issues facing our society and the consequences for the contemporary culture and the contemporary church (meaning local evangelical congregations) must educate themselves regarding Postmodern thought.

How do Christians confront the apostasy described in the world? What are the problems facing culture today? What do we Christians have to offer the world? In order to understand the issues, one must look to the unfolding of history and the ideas that have influenced our thinking and behavior. From any viewpoint, dramatic changes in culture occur when significant big shifts in ideas happen.

In a broad sense, there have been three intellectual shifts in history that have affected mankind:

1) pre-modern

2) modern

3) postmodern

Let's look at each period briefly and note the outstanding characteristics of each one.

I. Pre-modern Period - Institutions such as church and government were hierarchal and authoritative in nature.

A. *Government* - Headed by monarchs whose authority was supposedly derived from God.

B. *Church* – Headed by the Catholic Pope.

C. *Social* - Social position was fixed at birth; sons of lords became lords; sons of shoemakers became shoemakers.

D. *Education* - Traditional authority dominated the church:

    1) Very few people had an education.

II. **Modern Period** – The rejection of the Catholic Church authority; trust in individual or collective reasoning; faith in the power of reason is the major tenet of the modern worldview. With the cultivation of reason, man can expect progress in science and society.

A. *Protestant Reformation* – Doctrine of *sola scriptura* (scripture alone is the ultimate authority for the Christian).

    1) Put the Bible in the hands of each person.

    2) Each generation was to be drawn into a deeper spirituality by reading the Bible and passing it to the next generation.

B. *Scientific discovery* (demolished all previous scientific work).

    1) Nicolas Copernicus – earth moved around the sun.

2) Galileo – objects of different weights fall at the same rate.

3) Isaac Newton – completed theory of motion for both the heavens and the earth.

4) Darwin – evolution versus creation.

C. *Philosophers* – The modern mind began to question previous authority.

Prior to the 1600's all world views were theistic.

1) Rene Descartes – He believed in the mathematical scientific approach. Although he himself believed in God he asked questions such as, "Does God exist and can a soul be immortal. Can we know and understand our world?" He discerned to discover the laws that ruled the universe.

2) John Locke – Asked what do we know and how do we know?

3) Nietzsche- Believed that "God is dead." Formed the philosophical foundations for Nazism.

4) Marx- Developed the political dialectic of Communism.

5) Marcuse – Critical theory

6) Fromm - Psychoanalysis

III. **Postmodern** – No standard of truth; no right or wrong; replaces standards of resolute truth; it is all relative. The philosophy of "Postmodernism" is not a theory or creed: it is more like an attitude or movement, a way of looking at life. There are a few key components of the postmodern worldview that are discussed in this book:

1) Critical Theory

2) Dialectical Thinking

3) Negation

4) Social

5) Political

6) Theology.

Dialectical Thinking and Negation are major components of Critical Theory. Since there is no absolute truth in Critical Thinking one must use Dialectical Thinking as a reasoning tool in order to arrive at some truth or knowledge on any given subject. Negation is the act of taking one back to the origin of the problem. Critical Thinking becomes a new way of looking at reality.

Critical Theory was promulgated by a group of secular, German Jewish philosophers during the early part of the twentieth century and has had a major impact on all phases of European and American society. Their philosophy has contributed to the liberal, permissive and anti-Christian fabric of our lives.

Fueled by Marcuse, a leader in Western Marxism and Critical Theory, the 1960's erupted with militant student uprisings revolting against the Vietnam War, and any form of traditional systems all in the name of human liberation.

"The human mind," says C.S. Lewis, "has no more power of inventing a new value than of imagining a new primary color, or indeed, of creating a new sun and a new sky for it to move in."[1]

CHAPTER 1

CRITICAL THEORY'S NOUVEAU PROPAGANDA

The day after Christmas 2009, The New York Post writes under the headline, *"Crowd Ignores 5th Ave. Stab."* A homeless man was stabbed by another outside a Fifth Avenue church, where the argument escalated in front of St. Thomas Episcopal Church at 54th Street at 6:45pm. Kids in the passing Christmas crowd of tourists and busy New Yorkers were hardly traumatized. The police remarked that the victim was wounded in the chest, arm, and face, but his injuries were not considered life-threatening. One mother said of her children, who were with her, "'They watch a lot of murder shows and CSI, so they're used to it.' " What has happened? Has the loud roar of human cruelty toward others so desensitized adults and children that they are no longer affected by such horrific and traumatic occurrences? Is society becoming ethically and morally immune to beastly behavior? If so, why?

The ominous trend toward violence bares the consequences of a world seemingly ignoring the protective providence of God. Daily news broadcasters give us front row seats to the grim reality of a lost and dying world where once biblical moral and ethical values guided societal behavior. Humanistic ideals have speculated that men with greater insights such as the philosophical minds of modern times, Hegel, Marx, Horkheimer, Marcuse and others have given answers to the problems of humanity.[2] Much of their philosophy is based on the theory that teaches man is basically good, just dysfunctional and in need of guidance. Obviously man's sinful nature is attempting to hide beneath the secular wisdom of our time. On the other hand, biblical doctrine teaches that man has a sinful nature; as a matter of fact. Scripture teaches that we have a natural tendency toward sin (1 John 1:8). Lack for the pursuit of fundamental truths and understanding of resolute reality is leading to extensive worry, stress and misery—frantic culprits that are robbing and stealing mankind's peace. The treacherous thinking of modernity sadly leaves one watching in awe as society's treadmill becomes steeper and steeper with the consequences of the depravity from Godly principles.[3] In turn, the trend toward a superficial society is reflected in our everyday behavior as pride in self consistently walks its own way without dependence upon God.

No doubt, societal problems, past and present, have roots that stem from scientific and philosophical ideologies from the wisest of men, but modern principles have not lived up to their predictions in many areas. The First World War (1914-1918) and the Second World War (1939-1945) demonstrated to the world the massive amounts of human slaughter and genocide. While science had produced vaccines for polio and smallpox, it also saw the invention of nuclear bombs and weapons of mass destruction. And although the power of reason and science had become too great and vast, nevertheless the disillusionment of solving society's problems was strongly felt. Philosophical modernism was unable to eradicate the need for religion. The concern became that the hopes of modernism itself had failed.

Opportunists have seized upon social problems throughout history in numerous ways. Uncertainty of the future in a society always seems to beckon actions in new directions. The new direction leads away from modernity's existentialism (the idea of individual responsibility), into the arms of the current term, Postmodernism (PM).[4] Postmodernism challenges all human perceptions as a matter of a point of view allowing it the embracement of radical relativism.[5] The beginning stages away from modernism to post-modernism reach as far back and have defined roots in the establishment of the Frankfurt School or Institute for Social Research, affiliated with the University of Frankfurt, Germany (1923). At the institute a group of Marxist intellectuals who began a multi-disciplinary approach to solve the problems of modern society such as individuality, morality and personal freedom were testing different philosophical theories. The school's pervasive premise was to solve the societal woes of human development permanently. By transforming society to a new radical philosophical realm it would redefine man and aspire to create virtue in a society without the supernatural or metaphysical stimulus of faith and fear.[6]

Remarkably, a whole new mindset was exacting a place in history that would eventually redefine man, society, politics, and religion. The hope of the movement was that people would desire a society where man would live without any constraints to his, "freedom." Freedom would be the cry!

Don't tell me what to do and don't judge me! According to post-modern thinking, the ebb and flow of life would be shaped by societal changes based mainly on the reevaluation of Marxist philosophies, his concepts of social justice (equality and solidarity) and the use of learned propaganda[7] tactics in order to accomplish the required changes.[8] The liberal philosophy was intended to expose the human situation and its relationship to community; as opposed to an individual, in the varied areas of religion, law, state or government, and economy, including the entire spiritual and physical culture of mankind.

"Society does not consist of individuals, but expresses the sum of interrelations, the relations within which these individuals stand." Karl Marx

A clearer understanding of Marxist principles helps one to understand The Frankfurt School's philosophy of bringing social justice to the masses. Marx being dead but by no means forgotten established Marxism. The theory was set forth by Karl Heinrich Marx (1818-1883) and Friedrich Engel (both Germans) in the mid nineteenth century during a tumultuous period in European history – World War I. Marx, leader of

Classical Marxism and lead proponent of "Communism" otherwise known as, "Socialism" or Social justice claimed he was going to build, "a worker's paradise," heaven on earth – utopia." [9] In his written work, *The Communist Manifesto*, he announced, "The history of all hitherto existing society is the history of class struggles" (hegemony). His radical means to achieve his ideology was easily accepted because of the political upheaval in Russia. As Marx established in his written work, *Das Capital*, and other writings, old causes give way to dissatisfaction and this facilitates the opportunity to receive the popular support that favors change and the promises to cure all social ills. How did Marx formulate his concept of Marxism? His Marxist concepts were influenced by George Wilhelm Friedrich Hegel (1770-1830) who was the foremost philosopher of dialectical thinking (discussed fully in chapter 2) and Ludwig Andreas Feuerbach (1804-1872) philosopher of materialism. Marx took Hegelian dialectical philosophy and literally turned it upside down to create his concept of communism. His intention was to dethrone God and destroy the concepts of capitalism that he believed caused the disparity between classes of people. He made no bones about the fact that his philosophy would be the new religion. The people would worship, adore and give allegiance to the new government that would liberate the down trodden and level the playing field of wealth.

Tale-telling words from the modern book, *The Black Book of Communism*[10] in its foreword declares: "Communism has been the great story of the 20th century ...in the wake of the cataclysm of 1939-1945 it made a giant leap westward... and an even greater one eastward to the China Seas. With this feat...it had come to rule a third of mankind and seemed poise to advance indefinitely; for seven decades it haunted world politics, polarizing opinion between those who saw it as the socialist end of history and those who considered it as history's most total tyranny." The introduction of the book states that "...Communist regimes...turned mass crime into a full blown system of government." It cites a death toll which totals 94 million... and claims that communist regimes are responsible for a greater number of deaths than any other political ideal or movement, including Nazism."

Pulling from Marxist theories, the proponents of social justice concepts recognized that history revealed the use of propaganda dialogue could become an effective tool to manipulate and hold society captive to its ideals. During World War II, Adolf Hitler, (1889-1945) gave rise to the extremist Nazi party based on German nationalism and socialism. The party was partly fueled by the occult world stemming from mysticism in Hindu religious beliefs and Marxist ideologies. The major difference between Communism and Nazism based on slightly different totalitarian systems is that Communism is concerned about the class system while Nazism is based on race and territory.

Hitler became a mastermind of propaganda and used its effectiveness to promise peace, prosperity and liberation to the people. He had become acutely aware that at a time of upheaval in society, indoctrination to social changes becomes an open door for the ones seeking change. With little effort, Nazism's use of propaganda slogans was able to seize power over the press, the radio, the courts and the police. Hitler's obsession to be a world leader and his jealousy of the Jews, whom he believed wanted to dominate the world, energized the power struggle toward anti-Semitism. His propagandistic ideologies encouraged and drove otherwise humanitarian men to think nothing of slaughtering Jews, Christians and anyone that was considered weak and useless in his idea of an utopian world. [11] Hitler's personal quote is, "Always before God and the world, the stronger has the right to carry through what he wills."[12] Subsequently propaganda dialogue, obviously a destructive way of using words to describe a fictitious picture to someone, becomes the manipulative tool used by propagandists to guide the general population into different social behaviors. Clever use of propaganda presents a half-truth as total truth by manipulating well meaning words, words that a person would normally and naturally embrace. The propaganda words used in Nazi ideology are still being echoed today, but as noted they have reaped havoc in the past. History has proven that Hitler's ultimate dictatorship, his tyrannical government and entire success was due to the effectiveness of propaganda. He managed to dupe Western Europe.

Hitler's ascension caused Dietrich Bonheoffer, a Lutheran pastor and theologian who suffered during wartime, to write, "The paradox is that evil wears the mask of enlightenment, of humanitarianism, of historical necessity, of social justices." [13] He was forced to recognize that the infrastructure of politics was embracing Nazism and threatening the very existence of traditional Christian theology. Bonhoeffer substantiated his belief that Nazism was becoming a prominent force in Germany as he watched the people succumbing to the rhetoric of its lies. He wrote this example of how the people responded to the propaganda by using the analogy of a bull. The bull represents a revolutionist who upon seeing a red cloth waving at him fixates his gaze on the cloth and makes a run toward it. The bull is so enthralled with the red cloth that he does not see or hear who is actually flashing the cloth. Hitler's Nazism depicts the red flag with the swastika, known as a mystical symbol; a deception to the people perpetrated by his masterful demagoguery. Bonhoeffer was only thirty-nine years old when he was hanged by the Nazis for refusing to renounce his Christian beliefs instead of joining the forces of evil. Bonhoeffer continues to call from the grave for the awareness of the insidious evil that proposes social justice for individuals and institutions without understanding true justice. He realized that the use of propaganda dialogue caused a partial surrender of purposes by compromising truth, thereby creating radical changes.

"Honesty [Truth] is of pervasive human importance... Every social activity, every human enterprise requiring people to act in concert, is impeded when people aren't honest [true] with one another." [14]

Bonhoeffer described a short aphorism depicting radical changes versus compromise.

Radicalism hates time, and compromise hates eternity.

Radicalism hates patience, and compromise hates decision.

Radicalism hates wisdom, and compromise hates simplicity.

Radicalism hates moderation and measure, and compro-

mise hates the immeasurable.

Radicalism hates the real, and compromise hates the Word.[15]

Around the turn of the twentieth century, the broader perspective of new ideas in philosophy was being formulated by one of the Frankfurt School's theorist, Max Horkheimer, who became the director of the Frankfurt School in Germany. In 1937, Horkheimer[16] launched and defined Critical Theory (CT) in his essay, "Traditional and Critical Theory." He birthed the theory influenced by Western Marxism and the school's philosophy propelling it across the globe. CT states that,

1. "a theory dominated at every turn by a concern for the reasonable conditions of life;" (basic necessities of life such as food, clothing, housing and leisure.)

2. "a theory which condemns existing social institutions and practices as inhuman "(defined as Capitalism);"

3. "a theory which contemplates the need for 'an alteration of society as a whole'"(alternative reality).[17]

With CT, people are being offered a view of reality which is counter to the worlds' current scorned concepts which conceive freedom and reason as a state of mind based on right and wrong. CT's perspective is to change one's perception of reality in order to change society to one that is considered free from any restrictions of ethical or moral oppression. Under Horkheimer's tutelage this new prevailing world paradigm of thinking had the potential to change the landscape of any society. In other words, tenets belonging to CT change with the subject, allowing it to be applied to any particular historical juncture. Any cultural, scientific or religious premise will no longer be objectively true; therefore one's reality can be changed to one's own interpretation of life. To accomplish his theory, Horkheimer envisioned a panel of economists, sociologists, historians, and psychologists as a research team to study in laboratory experiments and to investigate social and political problems. The Frankfurt School's members created a theory, apart from a specific concept of thinking that has engendered spiritual and/or religious connotations. The theory proposes change occurring slowly and methodically by deconstructing and reconstructing truth, reality, concepts and ideals. With these concepts it is easier to take control of a country internally rather than with the external outbreak of war.

WWII found the Frankfurt School in opposition to Hitler's beliefs, forcing them to immigrate to the United States. The theorists such as Max Horkheimer, Theodor Adorno, Herbert Marcuse, Leo Lowenthal, and Erich Fromm continued their work at Columbia University in New York until the early 1950's when after the war, several of the theorists decided to return to Germany. Among those who stayed in America was Adorno, who taught at Princeton and at the University of California, Los Angeles. Fromm went to the Washington School of Psychiatry and co-founded the William Alanson White Institute of Psychiatry, Psychoanalysis and Psychology. He was also a faculty member at Bennington College, Michigan University and New York University. And last, but not least, Marcuse, a German Jew (1898-1979) and a revolutionary figure in the 1960's, taught at Harvard, Brandeis and the University of California, San Diego.[18]

The American mindset of Critical Theory was initiated and is accredited to the utopian Hegelian theorist, Herbert Marcuse, who achieved political influence in the 1960's. In the beginning stages, Marcuse and the Frankfurt School back in Germany collaborated to bring this paradigm of diverse thinking to the United States. In short, America would become the testing ground for Marcuse's theory. Could a great nation be transformed from a capitalist society, by transforming the individuals and their cultural institutions, to a socialist society?

Marcuse's ambitious theory took on a new, revised and revolutionary form of Marxism that was embraced by much of the world catapulting him into the position of "Guru of the New Left." As such, CT can be construed as a new type of atheistic religion. His writings and speeches on university campuses in the USA (as he continued as a college professor), tirelessly criticized any advanced industrial country particularly, America. The heart of advanced industrial countries, according to Marcuse, consists of an Imperialist system designed to overpower or dominate others.[19] He deemed Imperialism as sexist, racist, environmentally destructive, domineering and oppressive especially to the working class. According to CT the advanced industrial society would create a false need in individuals that would drive them into the current system of production and consumption. Marcuse's assertion was that the growth in innovative goods such as technology, research, and generally anything that would contribute to a perceived betterment of materialist goods would serve only to increase the appetite for the consumer. In his mind just as an addict is addicted to drugs, capitalism creates a form of bondage to the individual because the consumer relinquishes his individuality. For CT thinkers, human freedom is what food is to the body. Marcuse quoted, that, "Man, considered as a creature in the state of nature, that, is not restricted by civilization, is born free; yet in civil society he is always in chains or unlikely to be happy."[20] CT claims that the civil state will out of economic necessity create in its own strength a creative culture-forming force; personal happiness and rights that can only be obtained by the liberation of its current oppressive existence. Marcuse's resolution was to reach for recipients that would be ready for a radical change from a capitalist mentality to a socialist mentality. Accordingly, Marcuse felt in order to accomplish his plan the goal would have to be to form a post-Christian society by removing Christianity's supposed authoritative laws from the culture.

The younger generation in Western culture has demonstrated that not only can they be easily swayed by CT, but have helped to usher these changes in America's society. Because of the persuasiveness of CT, we had the backlash spurned by the Vietnam War and the counter-culture of the 1960's. Proponents of this era detested the materialistic and authoritative society and describe the counterculture as a celebration "... a rejection of endless consumerism, of rigid nuclear family suburban lifestyles, of sexual repression especially for women, of the fear of intoxication (except for alcoholic excess, still today the one officially approved recreational drug in American culture) of hypocritical church going and of the social ideologies that affirmed war, racism, and inequality."[21]

What would CT's perspective mean for a current society? It means a "renewed imagination of revolution (change via conflict) until all are considered equal - utopia."[22] As Marx represented the revolutionary fever of the past, the hope is that today there is another "Marx" that will deliver society from perceived oppression, injustice, and totalitarianism. Martin Puchner, currently a Professor of English and Comparative Literature at Columbia University, states that there is a call for a new "Marx", "…the Marx who knows that it is possible to articulate alternative worlds, alternative modes of organizing our world that is different from the one that is prevalent today. We need the Marx who sought new forms for writing and thinking."

In conclusion, the Frankfurt School's sole mission both here and abroad has been and still is to train proponents in the methods necessary for the promulgation of "Critical Theory as Critical Agents." Marcuse's followers' current concept of Critical Theory encompasses Hegelian, Marxist ideologies and social theories by reinterpreting them into a new perspective for the redefinition of man. This happens through the use of humanistic psychology, creating alternative reality, and for a frontal attack on ethical and moral values of a society. These concepts are used to disarm old patterns of thought in society and to destroy the concepts of right from wrong; thereby enabling the possibilities of creating an illusion of freedom. Unfortunately, immorality flourishes under this type of social setting. James Madison, fourth President of the United States and one of its Founding Fathers, cited the fact that a form of limited government is "wholly inadequate" without personal conscience as the internal social control..."

William Penn quoted, "If man will not be governed by God then they must be governed by tyrants."

CHAPTER 2

ALTERNATIVE REALITY VIA CRITICAL THEORY, DIALECTICS, NEGATION

*"Philosophers have merely interpreted the world in
different ways but, the point is to change it."*

-Karl Marx

Critical Theory's pervasiveness touches every aspect of our lives including the way we think, the way we live and the way we act out solutions to situations. In 1941 Marcuse published his book, *Reason and Revolution,* which introduced English speaking readers to Critical Theory and dialectical methodology of Marx and Hegel. It later provided the tools for Dialectical thinking. Substantial evidence will prove that both, Dialectical Thinking and its partner in crime, Negation, are equally integral to the understanding of the current concept of Critical Theory (CT). Negation and Dialectal Thinking are the reasoning or arguments driving CT in its effort to create and promote alternative realities. Together, this deadly combination creates such confusion of truth until the mind has no logical way of processing reality. Over the years, Dialectical Thinking and Negation have taken on many variations and continues to rest with the pedantic teacher and German philosopher, G. W. F. Hegel. As one group of writers put it, "Hegel's dialectic is the tool which manipulates us into a frenzied circular pattern of thought and action." [23] The definition of Dialectical Thinking is a process that denies absolute truths by circulating many different agendas until no truth has basis.

Recent headlines detailed a well-dressed gentleman from California who arrived at the entrance of the Pentagon. According to the security police he was seen reaching for what they thought was his I.D. but instead reached for a gun and started shooting at the police. Reasons for this behavior were inconclusive because it did not make sense. The shooter stated in written correspondence that he was confused about the reality of the 9/11/01 disaster; whether it had actually taken place or not. No surprise here, if he were educated in schools where CT influenced the curriculum, truth has no basis. If one was told that the 9/11 disaster took place and then was told that it never happened what choices would one have? One could accept that the 9/11 disaster as having taken place, or choose to believe that it did not take place and side with the nay-sayers or decide neither. Being totally confused one would like to believe all opinions are equally valid according to dialectical thinking. Conventional logic would label this gentleman as mentally disturbed which is eventually what happened.

Dialectical thinking creates frustration at best because how can one decide truth with such a see- saw effect of thinking? Obviously, life had become so fictional and illusionary for this person that he could not discern true reality. In extreme cases, underlying reality will be so illusionary that people will only see fiction and fantasy in everyday life. Imagine a world with such double mindedness. As can be seen, reality will become immersed in imagination, fantasy or fiction in order to create or invent other realities.

DIALECTIAL THINKING

We see dialectical writing, dialectical materialism, dialectical theology, dialectical psychology and dialectical schools. The primary premise of Hegelian Dialectical Thinking is used to cancel out absolute truth or neutralize truth, it all becomes relative. My truth may not be your truth but don't worry about it anything you chose to believe is true. By eliminating the "either/or's" in this type of philosophy, the individual would be considered freed from oppressive realities or authority. Dialectal Thinking dates back to the ancient Greek philosopher Hericlitus. The word, "dialectic" comes from the Greek word *dialektike* which means the art of conversation or debate. Originally DT was a concept of reasoning for the purpose of arriving at truth and knowledge on any given topic. But over the years DT has evolved to rest where it is today. As with all ideas there exist points of view that are good and some views that are bad. The primary tools used to achieve CT's thinking are propaganda tactics, unusual dialogue, consensus building, and if that doesn't work, terror and intimidation.

The formula for dialectical thinking is a complex formula used to adapt to various situations in order to advance an agenda, such as through a crisis. The steps taken to achieve one's agenda use the terms thesis, antithesis (an opposite position), and synthesis, creating a different solution to a crisis. In DT the synthesis is then confronted with an antithesis which in turn produces another synthesis. The process keeps repeating itself with yet another, yet another solution until absolute truth becomes unrecognizable. Therefore the formula allows for broad interpretations of truth where anyone's agenda can be met.

For instance, the Gulf of Mexico oil spill can be considered a crisis (thesis). This is a perfect set-up for manipulation if one wants to promote an agenda such as ecology. The antithesis in this situation would be no oil spills. Everyone agrees to no more oil spills depending on their agenda. For the jobless and those threatened by loss of livelihood, sanctions imposed on oil companies can destroy their way of life. For the ecologist, whose agenda is for ecological advancement, the synthesis is no more oil drilling, ever. So what is the truth here? It depends on your agenda.

The Yin-Yang symbol of Taoism can be a representation to illustrate Dialectical Thinking. The opposites are defined as the two parts (the black and white forms) but are dependent on one another as shown by a little black spot in the white form and a little white spot in the black form. The unity of the opposites is symbolized by the circle surrounding the forms; the process of movement and change, the way the objects relate (in unity and struggles) to one another to become a whole unit. Think of it this way by visualizing two individuals in a figure skating competition paired as a team that is described as "one man and one woman." The trainer advises the skaters that in order to win the gold medal they need to skate as the Yin and the Yang or as one. What does this mean?

Using DT, the skaters would have to see the weaknesses and strengths in each other thereby adapting every step and movement, giving the illusion of becoming one or a whole. Now to the average person watching the skaters skate, in one's mind, are they one and the same, or are they individuals? Let your imagination decide. The purpose of this exercise is that essentially they lose their individuality, becoming one and at the same time identical yet always considered equals, not individuals. In society, the individual or the identities of the whole become one as in an association of common laws, common interests, common rules, and a common religion. DT accomplishes CT's goal of obliterating individualism in favor of community. In the CT paradigm, individuality and uniqueness or specialness as an individual person is lost. Equality and social harmony will be the order of the day. With the concept of equality there is no hegemony or struggles between individuals where one can dominate the other.[24] Just as individuals in society or in a community relate to one another in its struggles and unity, these struggles and unity define the society as a whole and not the individuals according to CT. What will this produce? It will produce a global society or community.

NEGATION

Negation as the other aspect of CT denies the existing social order and refuses to accept any scientific premise (seen as authoritative) as truth or law. The process of negation strives to eliminate sources of power perceived as detrimental to one's state of mind. Negation dictates that one goes back to the source of the problem that has caused the tyrannical feelings that make one feel as a victim. Again a new way of looking at reality "Let's say we've got a black teenager in the inner city who just swiped the purse of a white secretary to get money for his drug habit…" CT "…will also want to look at the ways the woman actually contributes to the system that produces desperate teenage drug addicts. It is a system thing."[25] In other words, in conventional thinking who do you see as the victim, the one attacked or the one attacking? The answer will depend on the person's way of perceiving reality. If you are the secretary viewing yourself as the one victimized, you may be considered self righteous, dogmatic, and possibly a hate monger. To perceive the attacker as the victim, critical theory logic would dictate that he reverted to this behavior because of the prejudicial societal system that prevented him from succeeding in life.

As long as the authoritative societal system is seen as the power, the teen is deemed the victim. In this case, the crime of stealing is sourced back to the perceived system that caused the harm in the first place. The community will be held accountable for all the social issues contributing to the youth's sin. Again, the concept of negation is used to explain the sin by going to its source, in this case, society. One could wonder, "How will such controversy play out in the judicial system?"

Keep in mind that scientific methodology and common sense are DT's hated opponents for it abhors any framework of logic or reason. Let's say we are watching a television commercial. Ordinarily one would study the impression of the commercial on the viewers. Not so with the case of the negation principle. Instead the focus of research would be on the televised commercial, who is the advertiser, what power does it have, and who is the advertising company. The aim is to isolate the source of power because power impacts the viewer in a domineering manner according to CT. In opposition to conventional studies the process goes forward simply in order to gather knowledge to exact a positive change on the viewer.

One study that was conducted in 1971 by Ariel Dorfman and Armand Mattelart was to determine the effect of a Donald Duck comic strip on third world societies.[26] Instead of looking to see the effect it would have on such societies, the researchers studied the comic's contents to determine any imperialistic motivations of Disney Studios.

The question becomes, "If the oppressive societal system is so bad, how is it that people like Michael Oher seem to flourish?" Homeless since age two, he and thirteen siblings roamed the streets. His mother was addicted to crack cocaine, and he never knew his father. Oher states that he lived day to day doing the best he could. But a turning point came when Oher was sixteen. Briarcrest Christian School in Tennessee took him in as a "special need" student at the bequest of a benevolent well- to- do family. The next turning point came when the University of Mississippi picked him up as an all American tackle. He is now the subject of a book as well as a movie, "The Blindside."

In conclusion, Critical Theory with its underpinnings in Dialectical Thinking and Negation, deconstructs the traditions that once held us "captive" (as the elitist would try to have us understand), the beliefs that kept us grounded in our parent's way of life, our ethnic group, church, neighborhood and the general culture of life.

So far CT encompasses no absolute truths and no individuality; instead promotes community and equality, all Marxist principles. However secular premises cannot establish absolute truths because they do not feed the spiritual void in man. No amount of nourishment from a secular foundation will provide for a weak or withering spirit. In order to stand straight and strong, absolute truths are the structural support for the human soul of all societies. The foundation of absolute truths is the Word of God.

CHAPTER 3

WITHERING OF THE HUMAN SPIRIT

Somewhere, some place, some time someone said,
"It's a jungle out there!"

Most people will agree that times are changing with the widening gap between the dualistic world views in our societal, religious institutions, and their policies. Change and ethics have gone off the seismic chart hitting the Richter scale at a full "10." Once change constituted free love, Woodstock, bizarre outer attire, burning bras and the American flag. Today we have condoms for elementary school kids, anti-war chants at veteran funerals, gay and lesbian marriage, political correctness, the Ten Commandments thrown out of courthouses and activist judges. When confronted with the answers to these perplexing issues from Critical Theory's perspective, we begin to understand the emerging humanistic outlook.

Although our lives have been enriched with technological advances and opportunities, offering an improved standard of living, at the same time, society has suffered a severe blow. The by- product of such new secular philosophy as, Critical Theory, has caused a tendency for the withering of the human spirit. Take the disintegration of family for instance. Common knowledge shows that half of marriages not only in the secular world, but also in the Christian world, end in divorce. Consequently, an erosion of the traditional family structure has caused the primary vehicle for the passage of moral values from generation to generation to deteriorate. As a result of this finding there are families striving to maintain a "normal" family state as opposed to open marriages, domestic unions, and blended families.

Handing down wisdom, knowledge, and beliefs to the next generations through the concept of tradition within families was a support system that extended into neighborhoods, towns, and cities. Currently we see a disconnection by people, neither rooted nor aligned, to traditional concepts. Instead there is a tendency for self destructive behavior, drugs, violence, sexual abuse and the rise of suicide. It says that the type of change CT's proponents are looking for is the disintegration of the family structure. As promoted by socio-psychologist James Coleman in which he states, "In order to effect rapid change, one must mount a vigorous attack on the family lest the traditions of present generations be preserved."[27]

Currently, the family is defined by a recent Barna Research Group as "all of those people whom I deeply care about, and all of those who deeply care about me."[28] Under this grey shadow we see soaring out of wedlock births not only in the white community but also about 70% in the black community resulting in poverty. Inner city gangs form to replace the lack of traditional family resulting in children "raised" by children, and the growing influence of television, inner city culture, and the fad of the day. No direction exists.

Families are consequently not based on biblical doctrines but on feelings, i.e. whatever constitutes immense pleasure for the individual. Presently we have Generation M called the multitasking generation. Children in this generation have access to computers, I-tunes, MySpace, I-pods, Google images, texting and all this happens during their school home-work. Many cognitive scientists are alarmed predicting that all will not go well with these kids in the long run.[29] The problem is that over the last fifty years, education is being handed over from the local level or parental level to the state or federal level. Consequently, in the minds of parents the primary responsibility for the education of their children is no longer theirs. CT seizes this opportunity and at the educational level, supports the promotion that students should be "nurtured" rather than challenged. As a result, there are no academic achievement tests; instead students are moved grade to grade based on social potential. CT's aim is to make students into "critical agents," who are agents to transform society.[30] Public schools have become a hot bed for the indoctrination of students. As noted, the concept of CT examines all perceived powers such as government, patriarchal family, and Christianity seeing them as stunting the individual's growth. It strives to break the perceived powers down by destroying all credibility thus rendering them powerless and enabling emancipation from perceived persecution. In the United States, policies supported by this concept are being made to champion the rights of children; rights for children to divorce their parents, choosing their sexual preference, the right to birth control and abortion. A typical illustration of CT's non oppression theory is the hotly debated topic of euthanasia: *do we have the right to control when we wish to die?* The once highly held value of life uses the concept of CT to deconstruct and reconstruct the "value of life." Life becomes deconstructed in the sense that without God, man no longer has a soul. Critical Theory reconstructs man to be simply bone and tissue, same as an animal. Therefore, it becomes easier for man to destroy life. The impact of this flexible philosophy allows one to take possession of his life by releasing one from the supposed authoritative stance of religious morals. Critical theory needed Darwin's evolutionary theory to be true in order for their descendants who believe in eugenics - a selective breeding, the survival of the fittest, elimination of the weak in order that the strong survive.

Even if you are weary of life, you can choose to end your life as demonstrated by an eighty-six year old man in Holland who was not physically ill or in pain but simply tired of living and did not see any hope for the future. He was summarily assisted to commit suicide by a physician. The man perceived a reality which for him warranted suicide. The premise is upheld in Dutch courts where even sixteen year olds are granted the right to commit suicide without parental permission. Our own infamous Dr. Kevorkian and the U.S. Hemlock Society praised the Dutch and predicted that America will soon follow suit. In the case of euthanasia, Critical Thinking would leave society unable to make a judgment call for right or wrong. According to Critical theory, one cannot impose their absolute reality or truth (biblical truth) on man. As Pope John Paul stated in his 2000 Christmas message, "The temptation is becoming ever stronger to take possession of death by anticipating its arrival, as though we were masters of our own lives or the lives of others." One has to wonder, how far will the philosophy of Critical thinking push the eugenics button? Will it go so far as the philosopher Friedrich Nietzsche's estimation, "The superman can survive only by human selection, by eugenic foresight and an ennobling education...."[31]

With CT, the propaganda dialogue used to promote the relief of power and the right to decide for self continues in the academia field. The educational objective remains the same to teach against control. In America's modern society a familiar name to most is, Bill Ayres, who specializes in curriculum of education, instruction and trains future teachers. He has authored many books about educating children and parenting. His books include, *A Kind and Just Parent; To Become a Teacher; Resisting the Drive for Punishment in Our Schools; Teaching Towards Freedom:*

Moral Commitment and Ethical Action in the Classroom; City Kids; City Teachers, To Teach; The Good Preschool Teacher; and *Zero Tolerance.* Isn't it amazing that this is all from a man, who in a 2001 interview expressed his hatred for America when he stated, "What a country. It makes me want to puke." Bill Ayres was also the poster child of the counter culture of the 1960's. He was the founder of the Weatherman Underground who bombed the Pentagon and espoused such thoughts as, "Kill all the rich people. Break up their cars and apartments. Bring the revolution home. Kill your parents, that's where it really is."[32] Frightening words such as these were broadcasted to the general public. According to Ayres, the United States' history embodies racism and evil thereby necessitating the need for the philosophy of social transformation. In his efforts, he founded a "social reform organization" called the Chicago Annenburg Challenge (CAC) to bring about social transformation. The CAC enticed public schools to accept its liberal agenda compromising traditional principles of education.

Today, Ayres is a scholar setting policies in our children's educational system. He also sits on the board of Movement for the Democratic Society which is helping the "SDS," the Students for a Democratic Society (a communist organization from the 1960's), to reenergize for the purpose of intimidating conservative speakers on campuses.

Marcuse's idea that "human freedom is what food is to the body" has given one license to indulge in non-traditional morals and values without feelings of remorse. For example, gender is no longer looked upon in the traditional manner, rather one can choose after birth to change their gender to please themselves. Computers have aided in the promotion of CT by allowing mankind to escape from what is human and its perceived limitations. The role of women has been radically deconstructed from its original concept as nurturers for the family. Finally, the concept that language shapes thought is central to CT. CT firmly points out that changing the way people talk, can also change the way people think. Dialectical Thinking and Negation hide under the umbrella of Critical Theory and present a myriad of ways of looking at social contexts such as gender, technology, feminism, race and language.

QUEER THEORY

Judith Butler's (b. 1956) queer theory is based on the Critical Theory premise. Queer Theory seeks to dispel the notion that identities are fixed. To characterize or assume that the name, "woman" can be attributed to all women will be null and void. Queer Theory is not another name for gay and lesbian studies for it goes beyond homosexuality and the examination of normative and deviant categories of behavior. Identity development is explored and grounded in an understanding that all aspects of identity such as gender, sexuality, and race are interrelated. The question that persists and where studies are focusing is whether heterosexual epistemological frameworks used in research are conducive to gay and lesbian studies. Such studies may require research designed, implemented, and analyzed from a "queer perspective."

Another area examined is the incorporation of gay and lesbian literature in elementary schools up through higher learning institutions. The belief rests on the premise that all students should not be assumed to be straight. Basically Queer Theory suggests that gender is not determined by biology or judged by a standard of morality and truth. Thus Queer Theory challenges all fixed notions of identity in various, non-predicable ways.

CT attempts to offer us opportunities to indulge our fantasies without any sense of sin or guilt. The next theoretical concept may sound even more far -fetched, but in actuality it is alive and well.

CYBORGS

That's right, you heard us, Cyborgs. Who would have thought cyborgs would be described as a celebration to escape what is human, particularly gender and all its limitations. By downloading our consciousness into computers, we free ourselves from the limitations of the flesh, the weakness of our bodies and our senses. Kevin Warwicke, a scientist in England demonstrated in 2002 that by placing 100 electrodes into his nervous system he was able to link it up to the internet. Conducting a battery of experiments, he was capable of operating a robotic hand, a loudspeaker and amplifier. "In their" (cybercentric theorists) "vision, the future human is a cyborg whose consciousness and physical reality are dramatically expanded by pharmaceutical alteration, and genetic modification."[33] These transhumanists envision a future where discovery of new genetic technologies will lend itself to create radically diverse human skeletons or structures. "We can rewrite the vertebrate genome, redesign our global ecosystem, and abolish suffering throughout the living world."[34]

The "age of spiritual of machine" as it is described may look like a world where human beings are midwives for the machines. We could essentially create a "mind child." Recently a sci-fi movie featuring Bruce Willis called "Surrogates" gives a vivid description of the future with a redefinition of man and how it could possibly look. Sounds ridiculous but so did computers at one time.

FEMINISM

Recall CT's tenet of no individuality, but equality, an illusion that has redefined womanhood. In the mid-nineteenth century, the concept of feminism began to be questioned. The feminist movement known as the "first wave" mobilized to advocate equal rights for women, the right to vote and the abolition of slavery. Reproductive rights and birth control were also questioned as well as issues of sexuality and pleasure. Feminism opened the door to question the institution of marriage as well as women and children being the property of men. This was seen as the "tyranny of men." The movement continued until after WWI when women were granted the right to vote. A couple of early feminists include Lucretia Mott who was famous for her efforts in the anti-slavery movement and Sarah Grimke who advocated the idea that God's judgment on Eve in the Garden of Eden was God's prophesy of oppression of women by men.

It was not until the 1960's that a "second wave" of feminism came about. The majority of the activists were educated young women and girls unified in civil rights struggles and the radical counter cultural movements. The "second wave" questioned the status of family, reproduction and upheld sexual liberation. The movement was carried into the 1980's. Currently we are in the "third wave' of feminism. Feminism takes on an attitude where it examines and celebrates the difference between race, sexuality, culture, and class. A novel concept was born called the "politics of hybridity." The "new hybridity" is used to describe many contemporary women and girls (especially in the United States) who are comprised mostly of women of color, women with multiple ethnicities, various cultural experiences and classes. These women are the new generation of militant feminists. Most of the women grew up or were in households that experienced the second wave of feminism and were influenced by the movement. Although the idea of not being under male dominance sounds advantageous to most women, biblically it shows that it takes women off God's original path.

Yet there are black feminist who claim that black women are doubly discriminated against culturally and as such multiple black identities need to be recognized and allowed to express themselves. They determined that literature based on African-American experiences and written by black authors would accomplish this.

RACISM

Generally defined, racism is the domination of one group over a minority group for the purpose of exploitation of its labor, resources or both. The Greek civilization during the first century is credited for the birth of "colored" people slavery as opposed to CT's stating that racism is born out of capitalism. Racism functions on the ideology of inferiority which is supported by presumed biological deficiencies such as strength and intelligence. The ideology is required in order for the dominant group to justify and effectively exploit the minor group.

The discovery of America brought the concept of racism to maturity by the end of the 19th century. Perceptions of America's exploitation of vast natural resources led to the development of theories based on racial superiority and master-hood. Today racism is seen as a lack of support for marginalized people such as the poor, African-Americans, gay, lesbian, and transgender populations. CT avers that capitalism in a democratic society is the root of racism because in a democracy the majority of votes dictate the rules and the rulers of the land.

Dr. Martin Luther King, Christian pastor and civil rights activist who from 1955 till his death in 1968 exposed racial injustices in the USA, protested in non-violent passive resistance which earned him the Nobel Peace Prize. He left us an invaluable lesson on how to mend racial division and build a better, united world.

LANGUAGE

Language can be defined as a system of expression and communication via speech, signs or symbols of ideas or emotions between human beings. The first indication of language used in history was when Adam was asked by God to name the animals of the earth. In Genesis 2:19-20 Moses writes, "Now out of the ground the Lord God had formed every beast of the field and every bird of the heavens and brought them to the man to see what he could call them. And whatever the man called every living creature that was its name. The man gave names to all livestock and to the birds of the heavens and to every beast of the field..." The passage signifies God as the author of speech or language. CT presents a different version of language.

Semiotics is used by the Critical Theorists to set the stage for language effecting social change. Semiotics is the study of signs and symbols to explain language and communication, therefore semiotics involves a chain of associations of the mind which eventually seems removed from the initial sign, perception or experience.[35] For example, if one should say "dog," what mental picture comes to mind? One person may think of their own dog while another may have a mental flashback of a dog that attacked them in the past. One way semiotics is being used is with the government banking system. The attempt is to systemically change our mental image of banks and the current financial system at large. Banks were once considered a safe place that one can save their money for retirement, "a rainy day," or a future down payment on a house. Banks still remain safe but the mental images today portray banks as greedy, liars, deceitful, and untrustworthy.

Joseph Egar, a renowned music conductor writes about a universal language of music and contrasts it to the spoken and written language. He writes, "In the mouths of some, peace has come to mean war, law, and order means official violence, liberty means repression, and gaining credibility means telling lies. Small wonder that successive generations of young people satirize words, 'Cool,' 'crazy' and 'bad' mean good; 'freaky' and 'weird' have desirable connotations; 'outrageous' and 'awesome' mean especially favorable."[36]

In conclusion, as a result of changing paradigms of thinking, society is evolving from one of spirituality to sensuality. We have lost our individuality as a nation due to tenets of belief that we must be immersed in community, equality, pluralism and relativism. The emerging society of social justice without constraints of moral or ethical values will eventually be consumed by the trap of global citizenship and global economy. We will have lost our individualism as people and as a nation.

CHAPTER 4

POLITICAL SHIFTS

"Let every other power know that this hemisphere tends to remain master of its own house." [37] - John F. Kennedy

Although intellectual, political, and religious shifts are causing individuals to swim in unchartered waters, one should be undeterred in the quest for answers. America once considered a superpower, the nation that other countries attempted to emulate, is currently donning and developing concepts that have caused other governments to collapse. If we look back to Germany before Nazism, its economy was in shambles. Stricken with much political strife caused grid-lock and the big changes accomplished absolutely nothing but confusion and heartache. The people were ready for anyone who had a plan to pull them out the pit. They turned to doctors, scientists and philosophers.

Now the global community has realized these movements as an opportunity to usher in numerous socialist theories recognizing Critical Theory as the "theory of everything." In the past the pseudo-intellectuals quoted the phrase "knowledge is power." Today, the edict is "theory is power" and numerous theories persist – gender, historical, social, political and ethnic. Consequently, recognition of the many theories has been seized by the special interest groups such as ACLU, PETA, PLANNED PARENTHOOD, and MOVEON.ORG. Individually these socialist theories should not trigger enormous concern but taken cumulatively they can reap devastation.

The following tenets are taken from Marx's book, *The Communist Manifesto*. What is interesting is to find how many of the concepts have or are already being established in America.

- **Abolish private property and give it over for public purposes. Confiscation of all property from all immigrants and anyone opposing the government.**

Recently, in the news, a lady in Connecticut lost her home to Pfizer Pharmaceuticals who wanted to build a new drug manufacturing plant. The town where the lady lived saw revenue in the form of increased tax dollars. After a court battle the house and land was taken away from the lady. The lot now sits empty because Pfizer changed their mind leaving the lady with no home that had been part of her life for decades.[38] The Supreme Court has passed the imminent domain law that allows property to be taken away by the state for the purposes of "development."

- **Big taxes, using a graduated or progressive system. Centralize all credit and money, exclusively owned and managed by the government.**

According to Marx, these proposals can be filtered through to the working class in incremental steps, progressively taking all money and wealth from the business/wealthy class and place the economy and means of production (industries) in the hands of the government. Government is increasing their power in the financial institutions and industries in the name of "promoting efficiency and effectiveness" through more regulation and centralization of commerce and credit. The actions taken by the Federal Reserve, the Office of Thrift Supervision and the National Credit Union Administration to ban "unfair and deceptive practices" of credit card companies is generally considered a good thing.

Although "analysts note that regulators have stepped back from an emphasis on educating customers about what they should do, primarily through disclosures, in favor of telling companies and customers what they can and cannot do."[39]

- **No right to inheritance.**

Return of the estate tax is looming in the near future. Estate tax is imposed on one's assets after death. It would greatly impact family-owned businesses and farms where heirs would be looking at a tax climb of up to 55%.[40]

- **Centralize all forms of communication and transportation. Government control over business and all means of production.**

Four million small businesses will be affected by a bill known as the Employee Free Choice Act (EFCA) if it passes in Congress.[41] Control by the government continues with the bill which takes away secret ballots from workers voting to join a union. Additionally, the EFCA can effectively take control of free collective bargaining by unions and employers and give it to the federal government. The federal government in turn could regulate wages, benefits, and basically every aspect of business.

Government is considering action to put "some accountability and standards in place" in respect to communication.

The Fairness Doctrine currently being discussed among members of Congress is an attempt on their part to present fair and balanced information on talk radios. Owners of the radio stations, whether liberal or conservative, would have to have a representative from the opposing opinion. Fear abounds that this doctrine would stifle free speech.[42] This type of legislation would be just the beginning of government interference with the airwaves.

At the internet level, there is already a "White Paper" written by the Federal Web Managers Council in November, 2008. The White Paper states, "The new Administration should develop government-wide guidelines for disseminating content in universally accessible formats (data formats, news feeds, mobile, video, podcasts, etc), and on non-government sites such as YouTube, Wikipedia, and Second Life. To remain relevant, government needs to take our content to where people already are on the Web, rather than just expecting people will come to government websites. Having guidelines will ensure that we're part of the larger 'online information ecosystem,' without compromising the integrity of government information."[43]

The railroad industry falls under Federal regulation in regards to environmental clean-up, hazardous waste clean-up, pollutants and safety. Government can also regulate the economic aspect of the industry such as rates charged, services, mergers, and investments, including trucking, passenger bus companies, moving and overseas companies.[44]

- **Establishment of labor unions**

Labor unions are organizations of workers whose purpose is to maintain decent working conditions at their place of employment. The unions bargain on behalf of the workers for labor contracts that include wages, benefits, hiring and firing, disciplinary actions, and safety. One of the first major labor unions in America started in 1886 where cigar workers and various crafts unions united to form the American Federation of Labor (AFL). Today unions enjoy greater access to the White House and Congress. Their influence is seen in the Healthcare Reform Bill, the strong arm tactics to destroy the secret ballot bill, coercion of workers to pay union dues and in the Democratic agenda.[45]

- **Free education for all children**

The only thing that Marx suggested that is of any value to our society is free education for all children. However free education today comes in a different package from the traditional way we are accustomed to. CT encourages students to verbalize and write their own living experiences. This mindset moves the paradigm of the teacher as a "knowledge giver" to the focus of legitimizing the students' knowledge and experiences as the platform for learning. Students are not viewed as individuals but as "collective actors" within particular settings as in racial, cultural, class, gender, and historical which are imbued with particular problems, hopes, and dreams.

Education has been historically recognized as pivotal to one's understanding of himself as well to a good society. We are already seeing tactics used in textbooks by historical revisionists who through the use of omission and distortion, and vague words destroy existing facts. Even as we write this book, the general convention of educators held in the state of Texas each year are considering taking all references of the founding fathers, Paul Revere, and Christmas out of all textbooks because of religious affiliation. How is this really done? One approach is using the value free tactic which has the tendency to equate actions to avoid assigning responsibility or appearing to take sides.

One can see how education has been diluted. Let's take the example of Jay Leno. In an episode of his show he decided to ask pedestrians on a L.A street corner if they could complete the title to well known books if part of the title was given. Book titles mentioned were, "Pride and ....", "War and.........," Gone with the ....", etc. These are very common titles which you would think most anyone would know. But no! Maybe one out of five knew the answers even a Harvard graduate in English Literature did not know the answers! What is happening? A whole hearted effort is launched to criticize traditional concepts of education which are viewed as a form of indoctrination, oppression, conformity and submission to dominant values. An education system such as this one, according to CT, is organized in a way to reinforce divisions in society (the working class, middle class, the affluent). CT considers education is a social structure. As such it can be analyzed and studied in order to exact social transformation and ultimately liberation or freedom from the perceived oppressors. CT strives to describe the interconnectedness between the social structures as well as their contradictions. In doing so, Critical social theory maintains that underlying social structures can be anchored into a "new society."

Rhizomes and mass media are other social structures that are discussed to demonstrate how they can be manipulated to attain CT's goals for society. Critical theorists have long realized that mass media can be a powerful instrument to exact change in society. Adorno viewed television as a powerful mechanism of social control. Marcuse, on the other hand, theorized that mass media and technology could be unleashed and used as a powerful tool to oppose current capitalist forces.

Rhizomes

One of the structures in society is a horizontal movement involving the concept of rhizomes which is modeled after the idea of the potato root system. The roots (which are called rhizomes) grow out from a potato in a long complex root system. As they grow underground, the roots sprout into other potatoes, developing a root system from potato to potato. The interconnecting potato tubers make it difficult to determine a beginning and an end yet the whole root system is unified. Proponents of the rhizome concept as a societal structure state that a rhizome doesn't end, but is always in the middle, between things, inter-being, intermezzo." [46] As such, the rhizome evades any limitation and containment as in a certain political or ideological system. The internet is viewed as a rhizome. As computers are connected to other computers, networks of communication are developed. There is no particular origin of the Internet as it is composed of infinite links. Removal of one or several links, even large servers such as Yahoo, AOL, Google, even Microsoft will not affect the capacity of the other links.

Recently the government professed a desire to regulate the Internet. Congress is considering a "kill switch" bill. It would give the President power to shut down the Internet for at least four months without Congressional oversight in case of incoming Internet blockage efforts from certain countries. Concerns abound for such legislation could squash free speech and mimic China's policy to police the Web with coercion and censorship. Apparently the government has learned the concept of rhizome. The internet was cleverly used to promote the presidential campaign in 2008. It reached out to the young voters and also to grassroots supporters that in turn gave monetary support in undetectable amounts. Unprecedented monetary support was raised. Thus the internet demonstrates a new creative way to bypass any obstacles or powers that may thwart the intended outcome.

Critical social theory mindset is revealed in such theorists as George Gerbner. His colleagues and the at the Annenburg School of Communication at the University of Southern California studied violence in television programs and concluded that consumers of such programming are prone to depression and fear prompting them to, get this, **vote for right**

wing law and order politicians and to developing violent behaviors. These studies, although great subject matter, have dubious conclusions. Whose agenda is being played out in mass media? Who has the influence over mass media today? The so called elitist say, "Well if you don't like what is on T.V. change the channel." We respond by asking, "To where? It is everywhere!" There is no beginning, nor end, i.e. a rhizome.

Manuel Castells who is the Chairman of Communication and Technology, at the Annenburg School of Communication has authored many books on technology and society. He writes, "But power does not reside in institutions, not even the state or large corporations. It is located in the networks that structure society. Or rather, in what we propose to call the 'switchers;' that is the mechanisms connecting or disconnecting networks on the basis of certain programs or strategies. For instance, in the connection between media and the political systems."[47]

Media

Mass media can also be considered a rhizome in the sense that it sets out to undermine an existing society to one that embraces a different agenda, in this case, the CT agenda. For example in the case of the *Simpson* and *Star Trek* both shows continued to "grow and expand through their constant reemergence in new forms (in the case of Star Trek, spin-offs, novels, products, etc... for the Simpsons, advertisements, products, and the seemingly infinite continuation of the show). While both have expanded so far from the origin that it is nearly impossible to relate much of the growth in the beginning." [48]

In 1955, Marcuse prophetically stated that the family was progressively replaced by mass media as the dominant agent of socialization. He writes, "As early as the pre-school level, gangs, radio, and television set the pattern for conformity and rebellion; deviations from the pattern are punished not so much in the family as outside and against the family. The experts of the mass media transmit the required values; they offer the perfect training in efficiency, toughness, personality, dream, and romance." [49] Marcuse also noted mass media as a means to contain individuals, hence society, by the control of knowledge. Thus mass media is an instrument of manipulation and societal domination.

Today we see an increase of violence and sex portrayed on television. Forty-six percent of high school students in the U.S. have had sexual intercourse. Although sex in high school students is common, it was stated that teens wish they had waited longer to have sex which suggests a lack of Biblical truths taught in society.

In conclusion, we have presented only a few Critical Theories in social science, in gender, racism, education, and the media. The next chapter will portray and discuss how CT has even invaded Christian theology as deceptive and mischievous as the HIV virus. In researching this book it was astounding to find the implications of this malicious theory and its effects on Christian theology. We pray that what you read will be considered seriously and take it to heart.

CHAPTER 5

INFECTED CHRISTIANITY

(Liberation Theology)

An HIV virus has the capacity to enter the host's body unbeknown to the host traveling directly to its cell. Entering the cell, the virus works diligently and covertly effecting changes that the host is slow to recognize. Ultimately the virus changes to the extent that it becomes part of the host chromosomes and its genetic make-up (DNA) where it is free to wreak havoc at will. The DNA of the human being is its blueprint: what you are as opposed to an animal. Imagine if all aspects of man, such as religion, metaphysical, and philosophical underpinnings are tampered with to such a degree as to alter the mind and outcome of what was once considered reality, a Critical Theories' ploy. Man, reduced to a mere operational, manipulative definition or just a blueprint like a genetic code or DNA opens the possibilities for major manipulation and control. Man would now be considered as a rational and emotional being with free will but an entity that becomes an open target to be manipulated by the elite. As such, the soul is assassinated; man is no longer tied to God.

Liberal theology (LT) encompasses numerous radical proposals that are metaphorically representative of the HIV virus' ability to scope out and invade the body of traditional Christian theology. Critical Theory has disguised itself in the costume of Postmodernism, as in every other facet of society; thereby empowering the structure of LT without being noticeably recognized. LT's aim is to be free to experience infinite potential in whatever god one chooses, to restore a positive self-image, and a glorious sense of self-esteem. These actions further the cause of equality and community activism versus biblical principles as a whole. LT construes the teachings of Jesus Christ in terms of liberation from unjust economic, political, or social conditions for the poor." [50] Unlike the biblical perspective of covenant community where God is at the center of life, liberation theology's copycat system of community is felt as paramount to create social change both within the church and society. [51] Mostly it is a humanistic socialistic doctrine that started in South America for the plight of the poor.[52] Marxism was making great strides because of its emphasis on the redistribution of wealth which the poor peasants welcomed with open arms. After watching the colonial elite and their great wealth the peasants felt the Marxist doctrine was their opportunity to upgrade to a better way of life. Little did they know the true outcome, as in the dictatorship in Cuba and Venezuela. LT has deep roots in Roman Catholic theology although later criticized as false doctrine by the Catholic hierarchy because of the Marxist doctrine of revolution and humanistic philosophy.[53] The Catholic Church believed strongly in the practice of doing good deeds, but not with the approach of Marxist dogma. Under the banner of a post-modern concept of relativism—that all truth is equal, pluralism's stream of conjecture, LT is found to be flourishing, quickly becoming a universal claim both with the Christian as well as the secular world.

The ecclesiastical world is divided over the proper response to the challenges that have seemingly wrapped its arms around social justice's strategy of tolerance for unity of all religions. LT's disdain of orthodox Christian doctrine and that of other religions tends to blur religions, and the idea of pluralism of faiths takes precedent over any one religion.

Ecumenical unity is what Liberation theology seeks! D. A. Carson quotes from his book, *The Gagging of God,* that "Philosophical pluralism has generated many approaches in support of one stance: namely, that any notion that a particular ideological or religious claim is intrinsically superior to another is necessarily wrong. The only absolute creed is the creed of pluralism. No religion has the right to pronounce itself right or true and the others false, or even (in the majority view) relatively inferior." [54]

The persistent drumbeat to exercise tolerance has led to the obscurity of religions in the hope to foster unity of all religions. Is the goal being accomplished? One survey reveals that sixty-five percent of Americans between ages eighteen and sixty-four believe that the God of Christians, Muslims, Buddhists, and other groups is the same God but with different names. Exactly what Critical Theory philosophers and its proponents were planning, expecting and hoping for – obviously the day has arrived on our doorsteps. Partially, it appears that relativism has become the answer to the colliding religious worldviews in the attempt to coincide and keep unity with all other religious view. Once total pluralism has been accomplished little effort will be needed to be put into establishing a global religion that is spoken of in the biblical prophetic end times.

Although Christians are pronounced to live in a pluralistic society, does that mean we readily accept others religious views as absolute truth? How does this play out biblically? For the Christian to embrace other beliefs from other religions drowns out the gospel of Jesus Christ. It places one in the position that they have to choose to stay quite in fear of being seen as intolerant, possessing a rigid belief system or continuing to speak out on behalf of the gospel even if it means isolation from others and possibly persecution. But sad to say, even many pastors have taken the path of competing ideologies to accomplish the broad-minded concept of the unity of religions in the belief that absolute truth does not exist. Recently, Brian McLaren, a foremost advocate for the Emergent Church Movement (discussed fully in Chapter 6) coming through the back door of Liberation theology, was featured as one of five evangelical leaders who embrace a type of unity among religions. In his book entitled, *Holy Mavericks: Evangelical Innovators and the Spiritual Marketplace,* his understanding regarding converts from other faiths include, "I don't believe making disciples must equal making adherents to the Christian religion.

It may be advisable in many (not all!) circumstances to help people become followers of Jesus and remain within their Buddhist, Hindu or Jewish contexts... rather than resolving the paradox via pronouncements on the eternal destiny of people more convinced by or loyal to other religions than ours, we simply move on... to help Buddhists, Muslims, Christians, and everyone else experience life to the full in the way of Jesus (while learning it better myself), I would gladly become one of them (whoever they are), to whatever degree I can, to embrace them, to join them, to enter into their world without judgment but with saving love as mine has been entered by the Lord. [55] Words admirable of McLaren, but just to counter with absolute truth and staying scriptural we look at 1 Cor. 9: 19-23 where the apostle Paul states that although he became all things to all people he disciplined himself in getting to know his neighbors with restricted limitations. His goal was always to glorify God and bring people to Christ, he states, "I have become all things to all people that by all means I might save some. I do it all for the sake of the gospel, that I may share with them in its blessings." Treating others with love, respect and acts of kindness is without a doubt a part of the good news of the gospel, but Scripture is clear that without the knowledge of what Christ did and that acceptance, one is under judgment of God (Rom. 1:18, will perish 2 Thess. 1:9). The Christians' goal is always to tell of the good news of the gospel and as Paul win those to Christ (2 Tim. 1:10).

In the book *The Supremacy of Christ in a Postmodern World,* Timothy Keller, theologian and pastor of Redeemer Church in New York City postulates that the way churches are ministering to society is simply no longer effective. At this point according to Dr. Keller, "the demon is in too deep for your ordinary way of doing ministry." [56] His comment can explain Critical Theory's postmodern version of the virus that has infiltrated Christian theology. Why is this happening? According to Dr. Keller, there are three main problems that are challenging the Christian faith. The first problem and challenge is "Truth" perceived as a constraint or power play used by the person espousing it. Half truths are being articulated in order to redefine theology but they do not correspond to Scripture. Bold as it may sound, what was once deemed as myths are being heralded as truth and what is truth is being portrayed as myth.

One of the many methods used to convey these myths comes via the entertainment and literary business. For example, the confusion of truth and myths are portrayed in the book and later the movie, *The Da Vinci Code*. The author, Dan Brown, has masterfully weaved a tale of supposedly secret information about Mary Magdalene and her relationship with Jesus and clandestine guilds or societies. The thriller story seems to question whether the Biblical account of Jesus' life is actually true. The bestselling book presents the account as being really a ploy orchestrated by the powerful Roman emperor during Jesus' life and that the Roman Catholic Church was really trying to silence minority voices who objected to the book's version of Jesus' life. Obviously Critical Theory's tentacles have latched onto literature and movies as part of an inventive way to plant seeds of doubt into the minds of believers and unbelievers. Christians are called to be aware of these deceitful traps and step up to the plate to counter ploys of such deception. How do we counter these deceptions with the Absolute Truth? (Acts 20:28-30)

The second challenge to Christianity is that "Guilt or Sin" is increasingly being downplayed. Once again Brian McLaren's name pops up and he states, through a fictitious character, Neo, in one of his books, "The only kind of sin we want to focus on as modern Christians are the isolated individual sins committed by isolated individual monads:" (monad is defined as an indestructible unit or a simple and indivisible substance like the atom being the smallest substance in matter) [57]... "lying, having an abortion, indulging in pornography, taking drugs, saying naughty words." [58] Obviously a monad is considered a person without an awareness of all sins but only those deemed socially unacceptable. Recall the case of the black youth robbing the white secretary. The focus is not on the individual that commits the sin but on the sin of stealing. In doing so, "The issue is who is truly good." [59] Herein the task of responsibility is removed from the individual onto society as a whole, back to community. Consequently there is no accountability for one's actions, accepting personal blame or fault.

The third challenge is "Meaning." We have all experienced discrepancies between what one person means versus the different ways of thinking and talking about the same issue. Scriptures in particular hold the ability for misinterpretation especially the, "Message Bible", along with several others that embrace loose interpretations. Another is the Revised Standard Version Bible that leaves room for any and all interpretation. The wording has been so modernized that the literal meaning of Scripture can no longer apply. M. J. Kruger in his essay *"Sufficiency of Scripture,"* addresses the issue of deconstruction of language to suit one's theory.[60]

He comments, "Deconstructionism has relegated all texts to simply societal constructions – i.e., the readers own experience and perspective so conditions interpretations that there can be no one 'right' interpretation." The common assumption is that theological professors are experts in Scripture, but if Scripture is misconstrued to fit one's agenda think of the numerous amount of deception that can be generated to achieve the agenda. With these happenings absolute truths will be abolished from the Bible in favor of the words of God being simple stories and myths.

INERRANCY VS. INFALLIBILITY

Without the authority of Scripture, opinions of religious interest will be as numerous as the sand on the seashore. With the new perspectives in postmodernism and its entanglement in evolutionism, relativism, pluralism, naturalism, and historical criticism, how is it possible that the inerrancy of the Bible be maintained? Much has been written with debates on the inerrancy versus the infallibility of the Scriptures. The inspiration of God to the Bible writers versus inspiration to the reader is also highly contested. The debate over the three factors of divinity, humanity, and inspiration has become quite serious since the interplay of these three factors can seriously undermine Biblical authority. Inspiration is denoted as a human aspect. Whereas reasoning claims, "Where there was humanity, there could not be divinity in any fashion, and where there was divinity, there could not be humanity in continuous association with it. This drastically modified the sense of biblical authority" [61] The mindset as applied to the Bible would dictate, "...that its meaning is not relative to its author or authors, but relative to us and what we make of it and our reading is always socially located. Thus a radical version of the relativity of human language, one implies subjectivity and pluralism in interpretation, challenges the truth and the authority of Scripture."[62]

HIJACKED CHRISTIAN LANGUAGE

A demonstration of how language is hijacked by liberal theologians is written in an article, "Raising Resident Aliens." The diagnostic question they proposed was, "What makes your identity as a Christian?" The answer came from the following quote, "Resident-alien homes and communities must embody a whole different ethos. Practices of prayer and worship, daily lectionary readings, Christian artwork, structuring the year with the church calendar, and service to others can help young people find the identity as disciples." [63]

This doesn't sound bad. So what's wrong with the wording? Reading carefully you will notice that this is describing works, not Christ proffered gift of salvation through Grace. Instead as in most pagan religions, it teaches that man will be saved by works.

Sociology will play an important part in the face of philosophical changes as demonstrated by one of the leading cultural semiologist.[64] Roland Barthes (1915-1980) who professes that in order for a reader to grow there needs to be a release from the author. He is known for his notorious essay in 1968 where he proclaimed his concept of death to the author (a type of reader- response criticism). The essay explains that death to the author is death to the '...traditional, heroic Author' passing on his words of wisdom to a grateful and essentially passive public" [65] A biblical case in point is the word, Propitiation, (hilasmos - reconciliation, redemption) the heart of the doctrine of Atonement; that is the blood of Christ fully satisfying God's offended holiness. God cannot look upon man's sin. Propitiation is a sacrifice that bears God's wrath to the end and changes God's wrath toward us into favor; thereby making God forgiving toward us, propitious toward us (Romans 3: 25; Heb. 2: 17; 2 Cor. 5: 19; 1 John 2: 2; 4: 10). Scholars who prefer the word,

Expiation, an action that cleanses from sin, but includes no concept of appeasing God's wrath by substitution of Christ use this word in order to put a new slant on the interpretation. The new interpretation of propitiation states that there is no reason to take God's anger toward sin into consideration because God is just love, loving you in all your sins. Simply profess Jesus as Savior, by faith, without the repentance of sins and move on in church activities with your good works. Truly our conduct in Christ is intended to back up our commitment to our spiritual life. However professing Christ without repentance of sins is not all of the gospel message for God is just and righteous and must punish sin.

Not expecting God's wrath is a deadly assumption. A life of unforgiven sins separates us from a life of eternity with God. Theologian Ron Gruden states that, "The basic assumption is that God is a God of love and that it would be inconsistent with his character to show wrath against human beings he has created and for whom he is a loving father." What's important to understand is that without Jesus' death on the cross satisfying the wrath of God, one cannot fully understand the true meaning of love in the words: *propitiation* or *expiation*. The true definition of love is that God sent his only begotten Son to die for our sins (John 3:16).

Appeasement of God's wrath is taught all throughout the Old Testament. As the Old Testament is a fore-shadow of the New Testament we read numerous stories appeasing God's wrath by the sin-offering, the guilt-offering, and the day of atonement (Lev. 4:1, 6:7; 16).

In other words what is being implied is that when reading the Scriptures it is not what God says, but what it means to you – create your own story. Author David Wells, speaking about the recent trend in writing contextualized theologies has said that, "somewhere in the making of each of its works the fatal step was taken to allow the culture to say what God's story should sound like rather than insisting that theology is not theology if it is not listening to God telling his own story in his own way." [66]

Critical Theory's position in theology intends striking out words and meanings that have stood the test of time such as conquest, control, authority, hierarchy, submission, domination, and empowerment all in the name of equality, freedom and social justice.

The student of cultism then must be prepared to scale the language barrier of terminology. First, he must recognize that it does exist, and second, he must acknowledge the very real fact that unless terms are defined...the semantic jungle which the cults have created will envelop him, making difficult, if not impossible, a proper contrast between the teachings of the cults and those of orthodox Christianity.

-Walter Martin

The danger will exist in the terminology used by the perpetrators because the dialogue will sound familiar but the meanings will be very different. Recently in a nondenominational reformed faith discipleship class students were asked to underline key words in this statement that would lead them to growth, "Content in relationships because you are accepted by God." Acceptance of the word, content would imply any or all relationships even ones that are outside of God's ordained relationships. Yes, we are all accepted by God after repentance of sins. But the word content is so broad that it allows for many interpretations which is exactly the aim of CT. Another statement within this study was a phrase, "Not fearful of God." Totally contradictory to the Word of God that states, "The fear of the Lord is the beginning of knowledge..." (Prov. 1:7). To question, argue, modify, or change any wording in the Scriptures is to disbelieve or disobey God. By calling into question the absolute authority and truthfulness of the Bible, the door opens up for man to essentially act as God as he interprets the Scripture at will. Because of LT's movement one must ask, "Are fundamental Christians becoming an endangered species?"

C.S. Lewis once stated that Christians must ask themselves two questions. "1. Have I been keeping abreast of recent movements in theology? 2. Have I stood firm (*super mostratas vias*) amidst the winds of doctrine?" [67] Although both questions are quite relevant today, the second question is the most significant.

In conclusion, by exposing the unfruitful deeds of darkness and effectively evangelizing and proclaiming "the Christ" to a lost and dying world we are providing the antidote to this insidious virus (1Tim.4:16). As we increasingly make use of the gained knowledge of secular philosophies, it becomes the duty of all Christians to prepare to answer the questions posed by the world. Questions asked by individuals that concern the differences between secular worldviews and that of a biblical stance. In other words, do not yield to the winds of doctrine by ignoring them, but fight back by learning the truth of the Word in areas of heaven and hell, creation or evolution, resurrection of Christ, life after death, universalism, is hell on earth, why does God allow suffering and use the correct answers essential to reason with others (Isa. 1:18). Churches must set the agenda in biblical truth in order to defend their faith or watch as they are swallowed up by the radical change of a new type of emerging church or by new ruling governments.

Teach me, O Lord, the way of your statutes;
and I will keep it to the end.
Give me understanding, that I may keep your law
and observe it with my whole heart.
Lead me in the path of your commandments,
for I delight in it.
Incline my heart to your testimonies,
and not to selfish gain.
Turn my eyes from looking at worthless things;
and give me life in your ways.
Confirm to your servant your promise,
that you may be feared.
Turn away the reproach that I dread,
for your rules are good.
Behold, I long for your precepts;
in your righteousness give me life!
Psalm119:33-40

CHAPTER 6

THE RAVAGES OF THE DISEASE

"Take no part in the unfruitful works of darkness. But instead expose them" (Eph 5:11).

M any evangelical church leaders have been completely caught off guard by Critical Theory's effect in the postmodern world. Nevertheless it is moving at breakneck speed through numerous offshoot movements of Liberation Theology pulverizing foundational doctrine as it goes. A steady progression of pluralistic ideas and socialistic theories have been tiptoeing into and, as of late, are blatantly tromping into theological textbooks and ecclesiastical writings. Liberal theologians, the World Council of Churches (WCC), the Emergent Church Movement (ECM), and the

Ancient-Future Movement (AFM) are currently thriving from postmodernism's toes dipping into liberation theology's wellspring of radical ideas.[68] Relativism continues to be the springboard lifting the different movements, higher and higher.

Despite the normative, historical position of the WCC in which it once solely embraced the unity of faiths and philosophies within the Christian realm, they too are working under the social banner of good will for all—social justice. They find themselves advocating for the unity of the church under the umbrella of the unity of all mankind and all other religions; again that wonderful concept of global peace—utopia and utilitarianism. Authors who embrace socialism have obviously snared their attention. One book that engaged WCC is by, Hans Kung, *Global Responsibility*, where he pushes the aphorism: "1) No human life together without a world ethic for the nations 2) No peace among the nations without peace among the religions 3) No peace among the religions without dialogue among the religions." [69] Such ideas and philosophies as these are concepts adopted by Liberation Theology, and are simply more proof that humanity's failure and departure from God's Word has allowed cultural pressures to seize a prominent place in Christianity.

THE EMERGENT CHURCH MOVEMENT

The ECM comprises a loose coalition of churches that came together in the early 1990's. ECM is skeptical of power and its structures so much so that they are all about CT's concept of deconstructing traditions and pulling people together as in a community atmosphere for social justice's idea of good works. One must understand that proponents contaminated by a CT mindset have taken hold of Biblical principles that are the bedrock of Christian faith and reinterpreted them using a postmodern value system. Tolerance, diversity, equality and "Gnostic" mystery have replaced once cherished biblical values such as sound doctrine, assurance, truth and conviction.

Presently ECM proponents are having seminars, writing books, creating websites and holding conventions in order to network church leaders with resources in the form of new ideas, and provide effective tools for the advancement of the ECM theology.

The originators of this movement include Doug Pagitt graduate of Bethel Seminary, Tony Jones, PH.D., National co-originator and graduate of Princeton Seminary, and Brian McLaren who graduated with a Masters of Arts in English, Magna Cum Lauda. Certainly, accolades that are not considered chump change in any one's estimation. But still do intellect and academic acumen make what they say true? The aforementioned trio has joined forces to introduce their antagonist's opposition to conservative Christianity. Paul Wells, professor of Systematic Theology in Amsterdam writes in his essay, *The Doctrine of Scripture: Only a Human Problem*, "It seems to me that our post-industrial times require us to ask new questions, questions that people 100 years ago would have never thought needed asking. Could it be that our answers will move us to re-image the way of Christianity (deconstruction and reconstruction) in our world? Postmodern deconstruction, when it arrived, was like a little gangrene setting in on the festering [Achilles] heel. If the new perspectives in anthropology linked to a dynamic and functional view of man provided an incentive to reconsider the nature of the humanity of Scripture, philosophies of deconstruction make it absolutely essential in a changed context." [70,71]

Doug Pagitt's comment is a tell all conclusion of the mindset of the ECM, "Perhaps we as Christians today are not only to consider what it means to be a 21st Century church, but also- and perhaps more importantly what it means to have a 21st Century faith. The answers to all these questions will have an impact on how our faith communities (community) are structured... and even how we understand the gospel itself."[72]

ECM's theology could be considered doctrinally minimalist and moving away from systematic orthodoxy. Leaning more towards cultural and generational mores, they are opposed to doctrinal structure that would restrict their actions. The emergent belief has derived one of its root systems based on George Lindbeck's (from the "New Yale Theology") proposal of viewing Scripture that does not require belief in the actual truthfulness of its language (relativism). In other words he asserts, "... the propriety of the biblical word as a foundation for theology and then [goes] on to say that the meaning of the Word is not self-contained but must be ascertained from the community of faith. This is precisely the theological methodology of the emergent church movement."[73] Theology has essentially been reduced to "Scripture and experience."[74] In other words, instead of what the Scriptures speak into your life as divine mandate, it will be whatever a person's life experiences lend to the Scriptures. Brian McLaren further states that the Bible is "not a look-it-up encyclopedia of timeless moral truth." At this point one may doubt the veracity of the Bible. Mr. McLaren will assure you that you have. He states, "...there is more than one way to 'kill' the Bible. You can dissect it, analyze it, abstract it. You can read its ragged stories and ragamuffin poetry, and from them you can derive neat abstractions, sterile propositions, and sharp-edged principles."[75]

McLaren believes that the doctrine of atonement should be thrown out because people today do not believe in sin. The authors of the book, *Recovering the Scandal of the Cross*, state, "God takes on the role of the sadist inflicting punishment, while Jesus, in his role as a masochist, readily embraces suffering.[76] According to the authors, the church should abandon the concept of substitution for our sins. Although the ECM does place emphasize on the incarnation and humanity of Jesus, they overemphasize incarnation/humanity rather than the exaltation of the divinity of Jesus Christ.

McLaren's enlightened worldview leans to the political left with the envisagement of health care coverage for all, ecological concerns, green energy and peaceful negotiations; in other words the social justices of "community-shalom-utopia." McLaren rests and lingers in 1 Corinthians where the church principles focus strictly on God's love skipping right by such issues as church discipline, the resurrection, sexual immorality or warnings of idolatry. His concern is not so much with the doctrine of Scripture as the practice of Scripture bound in the person's good works. He asserts, "We place less emphasis on whose lineage, rites, doctrines, structures, and terminology are right and more emphasis on whose actions, service, outreach, kindness, and effectiveness are good."[77]

Does this sound all too familiar to the very first deception in the Garden of Eden? "Did God really say?" Is the ECM movement just another cover up to promote good works over repentance of sin? We should all heed the words of the apostle Paul, "...If you think you are standing firm, be careful that you don't fall" (1 Cor. 10:12).

The message of the ECM is complex and simple at the same time. Emphasis is placed on being just like the human Jesus: kind, caring, for the poor, loving, and compassionate. Concurrently the movement has obliterated sin, hell, inerrancy of the Bible, deity of Christ, God's sovereignty, atonement, faith and worship, God's glory and thrust to save the lost. Can we honestly call this Christianity?

A former leader of the ECM, the Pastor Mark Driscoll, describes his experience with the movement by stating, "As soon as they started, that's when I started to having some friction... they were looking at things like open theism, female pastors, dropping the inerrancy of Scripture, penal substi-

tutionary atonement, literal hell, those kinds of things...
Once Brian McLaren was brought on to travel and speak
for us, that's when I hit the eject button."[78] We can't say this
enough. Once again this movement uses CT to seek to deconstruct and reconstruct the already foundational written Word.
Driscoll maintains, "...remember the emergent church is the
latest version of liberalism. The only difference is that the
old liberalism accommodated modernity and the new liberalism accommodates postmodernity."[79]

One may ask, "Is this just a fad?" Need more proof?
Listen to only one of the numerous liberal pastors espousing
the changes in theology. The popular television pastor, Robert
Schuller of the Crystal Palace in California, asserts, "I don't
think anything has been done in the name of Christ and under
the banner of Christianity that has proven more destructive
to human personality and, hence, counterproductive to the
evangelism enterprise than the often crude, uncouth, and
unchristian strategy of attempting to make people aware of
the lost and sinful condition." [80] Dr. Schuller's show pro-
vides an hour of entertainment oftentimes with Hollywood
type celebrities, beautiful music and words that ooze with
love. Dr. Schuller's believes that the soul that sins, shall not
die, but live eternally. Are we being completely taken back

to the Garden of Eden? Wasn't the same message offered to the disobedient Adam by the great deceiver – Satan? Christ's answer to this way of thinking, man without conscience, is found numerous times in the Bible. The Scriptures speak volumes in Ezekiel 18:20 "...The soul who sins shall die..." while Romans 6:23 supports this verse with the following words, "For the wages of sin is death; but the free gift of God is eternal life through Christ Jesus our Lord."[81] According to Scripture, Dr. Schuller's message will not provide salvation but definitely feeds the flesh by granting a momentary sense of relief from a possible sinful conscience. Paul warns in Galatians 1: 8, "If we or an angel from heaven should preach a gospel contrary to the one we preached to you let him be accursed." The alternative message of Critical Theory portrays Jesus as a Hollywood type hero who is not prone to violence and is not judgmental or condemning. He did not come to save people from hell but to live a life seeking peace, especially for the weak and down trodden.

No doubt it appeals to the carnal mind to believe the universal concept that all "dogs go to heaven," (universalism- everyone goes to heaven) instead of remotely thinking that someone may go to hell. But does Scripture tell us that insidious behavior takes us to heaven? The world renowned

Biblical scholar, Dr. R. A. Torrey who is qualified to examine the subject quotes, "I claim to be a scholarly preacher. I have a right to so claim. I have taken two degrees, specializing in Greek, in one of the most highly esteemed universities in America. I have also studied in two German universities. I have read the Bible in three languages every day of my life for many years. I have studied a large share of what has been written on both sides of the question of (Hell) in English and in German. I have written thirty or forty different books which have been translated into many languages. Yes, I believe in scholarship and I believe in the old-fashioned doctrine regarding Hell." [82]

In the here and now as well as the hereafter, no amount of secular education or financial wealth will atone for sin. A society without the constraints of moral law and the accountability for each individual action of sin allows for any and all crimes to be permitted without any thoughts to retribution in the hereafter.

ANCIENT-FUTURE THEOLOGY

Another offshoot of LT was initiated by Robert E. Webber father of "Ancient-Future Theology (AFT)." He was a Wheaton college professor for three decades and in his book, *Ancient-Future Faith Rethinking Evangelicalism for a Postmodern World,* (considered a primer for most postmodern Christians) he envisions a "new evangelical awakening." [83]

Webber advocates a return to first-century faith that originated with the apostles and later was continued by Catholic Church fathers. While the ECM disavows the Word of God, the AFT wants to add to the word of God. One only has to look at the lives and writings of the early bishops of the Catholic Christian church to observe the heresy in much of their thinking. The AFT would add to these ancient church fathers, thoughts of mystics, hermits and nuns. The methods of AFT are to subvert the Word of God by using experientialism, subjectivism, mysticism, and dominionism.[84] Webber postulates that early writings especially from second century Catholic Church fathers insights need to be recovered and studied by evangelicals. Webber stated, "Theology is 'an adventurous exploration of new horizons'. Theology is more like a 'mysterious adventure than a mathematical puzzle.'" [85] Sounds like a lofty definition of theology but theology described with connotations of mystery, adventure and uncertainty is not biblical. As if to contradict itself, this movement issues a call to go back to those Christian traditions and Christian history. On May 1-3, 1977, before his death, a conference was held in Chicago arranged by Robert E. Webber, "to draft an appeal to Evangelicals which would stress a recovering of theology, practice historic Christianity, and call them to a Christianity truly Catholic and Evangelical."[86] It was to be named, "The Chicago Call." The diagnostic question that begs to be answered is, "Why in one breath traditions of any kind, including the church according to CT are deconstructed, then in the next breath is a need to examine the early church and its founding fathers, monks, nuns, and Roman Catholicism?" Ancient-Future theology's quest is to get to the root of the "evangelical spirit," as opposed to what is revealed in the book of Acts and what the Lord has revealed through Paul. In liberation theology, practices of the Roman Catholic Church's desert fathers and Eastern Orthodox mysticism will rule and reign.[87]

Is there a call to go back to pre-reformation Christianity? AFT uses Critical Theory's concept of negation to take us into past church history instead of forward to the apostles seated at the feet of the original "Great Teacher." Going backwards to a time when the early church was Catholic and wrought with rituals, ceremonies, pagan practices and customs, instead of going forward in faith as in the process of sanctification, AFT wants to go backwards as in negation to the source of desert monk spirituality to atone for sins. In this case, the source is not the Word of God, but bondage through church ritual, ceremonies and works piled so high that the light and truth of the Gospel will be buried underneath the rubble for some time. The source of power is the power of bondage that will be placed on people if they follow Ancient-Future theology. As exhorted in the journal, *Christianity Today*, "Embrace symbols and sacraments. Dialogue with the 'other two historic confessions: Catholicism and Orthodoxy. Recognize that 'the road that is the church's future is through its past.' And break out the candles and incense. Pray "Lectio Divina." Tap all the riches of Christian tradition you can find."[88] Yes, "learn the crucial power of the church...as the powerful, untamable, Spirit-driven, Mysterious Body of which Paul spoke."[89]

What 'treasures' can the early fathers of the church have other than what is stated in the book of Acts? As R. Kent Hughes states in his book, *Acts. A Church Afire*, he describes the Book of Acts as "...a book with a splendid theme, tracing the work of the Holy Spirit through the birth, infancy, and adolescence of the church...Acts forms the perfect counterpart and contrast to the Gospel. In the Gospels the Son of man offered his life; in Acts the Son of God offered his power. In the Gospels, we see the original seeds of Christianity; in Acts we see the continued growth of the Church. The Gospels tell us of the Christ crucified and risen; Acts speaks of Christ ascended and exalted. The Gospels model the Christian life as lived by the perfect Man; Acts models it as lived out by imperfect men." [90]

"The study of the book of Acts is particularly important to the Christian because it teaches us how to experience a stimulating, exciting life, in other words how to make our lives count."[92] As Dr. Hughes notes the synthesis of the Gospels and the book of Acts is the uniting of all hearts of believers. Substantiated by Paul in Acts 4:32, he states, "Now the full number of those who believed were of one heart and soul…"

No truer words can describe what's happening in the transient theological world. It is not a "…yellow brick road [that] led Dorothy and her gang to self-knowledge…"[92] In fact it is outright dangerous to believe in this Wizard of Oz myth for it forsakes caution in regards to biblical interpretation and theology. No doubt Christianity is fundamentally dependant on history especially in regards to Jesus' life and what Scripture has to say. But as C.S. Lewis once wrote "the present occupies almost the whole field of vision. Beyond it, isolate from it, and quite unimportant, is something called

'The Old Day'...."[93] Yes, the good deposit in the Christian is Christian history as the foundation of one's faith. Certainly, if the Christian is amnesic about Jesus' life and what He did for us, about our Christian ancestors, the apostles their trials and tribulations, how can the Christian define himself? Presently it appears that Christianity is becoming less sure of the deposit. A foundational "deposit" is the cornerstone for truth (2 Tim. 1:13-14). If there is no foundation, there is likely no truth. The message promoted by CT and its offshoots is that God is love whose grace covers all sins, truth but only a half-truth. We should learn to be like Jesus and emulate his life on earth, be kind and take care of each other, including the poor and the environment. But Jesus is more than a model for living and the initiation of social justice. All noteworthy concepts, but Christianity celebrates the divinity of Christ as well.

In conclusion, history repeats itself once again as Christian Theology is under attack by Liberation Theology's super apostles, who preach another Jesus, from their postmodern influence upon religions fundamental theology (2 Cor. 11). Christianity is being reinterpreted as stated through a cultural grid that uses Critical Theory's paradigm of thinking to influence Liberation theology. The classic terms used in Christian theology are being restated in postmodern vocabulary by wearing the resemblance of divine clothing. The newly dressed words are presented to Christian society without the knowledge of foundational truth; the words that weave the web of destruction. Theology based upon God's unique revelation of Himself through Jesus Christ will be reinterpreted, restructured and replaced with a theology founded on humanness, with all its prejudices, preconceptions, desires and passions!

"The theological openness of [these] theological lone ranger[s] is itself highly attractive to the ethos of PM subjectivism."[94]

CHAPTER 7

A SUPERFICIAL SOCIETY

"When the idea of God is gone, a society will 'transcendentalize' into something else, some other concept in order to appear morally and spiritually superior." Alistair McGrath

The superficial society will be marked by partial knowledge and no genuineness or realness to ones' actions. The consequences of Critical Theory's prototype of a post-Christian society are supporting of these actions. First and foremost, citizens of communities will function as agents of change without the moral compass of the laws of truth set by Judeo-Christian faith. Where upon any society whose existence was once established on rational foundations of logic, truth, and reason will ultimately be contrasted by the creation of a type of alternative reality. Alternative realties extend a hand to a populace that seeks no limitations, no boundaries to moral values or ethics. Participants engaged in this reality turn their heads away from what was once considered sins of humanity. Furthermore, realities created without substantial truths will only enable individuals to falsify and disguise men already debased in transgressions; consequently taking sin to the next level. An overflow of effects such as deception, confusion, and paranoia will be leaders of the pack in promoting and uniting the new realities. As a result, the dawn of a superficial society surfaces replacing the standard of decency and God's intervention that was once maintained by humankind. The Swiss psychiatrist Carl Jung said it this way: "He warned us that the evils of primitive man are still crouching in all of us, alive and ugly in the dark recesses of the heart under the thin veneer of civilization. He said that only Christianity is keeping them in check; and if Christianity is neglected, the old horrors will sweep in again like roaring global flood. [95]

Around the globe the bombardment of CT's theory has reduced logic into theories, concepts, and suppositions based on feelings, emotions, and experience instead of sound conventional reasoning to determine solutions. Subsequent generations will move forward believing that as long as they are sincere in their feelings and emotions, then it must be true. In other words if it feels good, do it! When this happens, human reason is assassinated by removing the rational faculties of the mind that had previously distinguished the intellect of man from that of beastly behavior.

When societies' Judeo-Christian foundation is rendered weak by the erosion of the winds of different tenets it can easily be toppled for a time. The secular or religious structure may appear powerful and real on the surface; however, a foundation without truth is a flimsy, false structure. Consequently a thoughtless society emerges out of the shadows of obscurity to produce one without restraints, one that ignores the still small voice of an inner conscience and one altogether void of right and wrong. Simply put, a civilization veneered with only an appearance of the real and genuine can only yield a shallow superficial society which considers itself morally and spiritually superior. What constitutes morality in the minds of those in an alternative society? Josh McDowell nailed it on the head when he said, "…most of what people call morality today is simply pragmatism. 'If we don't condemn what the Nazis did,' people reason within themselves, 'what's to stop someone from doing it to us?' And they are right, of course; they recognize the need for objective morality, but cannot arrive at a true moral code-because they refuse to acknowledge the original." [96] Pragmatism is part of the erosion of the religious structure carried through in the sense that thoughts or ideas are valued solely in their practical observations of a secular society versus a society based on Biblical structure. The world is dehumanizing societies in different countries by increased abortions, commercialization for the children and nothing more than old age homes that simply act as warehouses for the elderly.

An unsuspecting society of social pragmatism can easily fall into a trap of injustice and immorality as witnessed during the Nazi era. Whatever was said by the leader and what was enforced by his supporters produced a society that acted without thought to a code of ethics. The thoughtless group constituted obedience, loyalty to the leader and government, and respecting all its laws and orders. They served the leader and government for causes that the masses believed served as a practicality to benefit the populace.

German Nazis in WWII exterminated people without guilt by the murderers who carried out their duty. For instance in the trial of Adolf Eichmann (known as the architect of the Holocaust) which began in 1961, he maintained that he was only following orders. The trial held in Jerusalem (as he was captured in Argentina by Israeli Security Service) brought to the international forefront the atrocities committed by the Nazis. Eichmann's role in the Nazi regime was to facilitate the expedition of millions of Jews in Europe to ghettos and extermination camps in Nazi controlled areas of Eastern Europe. Upon his capture he was charged with fifteen criminal charges that included crimes against humanity, crimes against Jewish people and membership to an illegal organization. But what was most disturbing about this trial is that Eichmann who was examined by a psychiatrist was deemed perfectly sane! That is amazing in light of the fact that people that commit atrocities such as genocide are presumed to suffer from at least some degree of post traumatic stress disorder if not completely considered insane. But without remorse, he stated in his trial that he was only following orders from his Fuhrer. Therefore, the horrific acts were able to be performed by a person considered mentally sound. Obviously in Eichmann's mind, he felt morally and spiritually superior to any established foundational truths. His belief system legitimized the brutal acts. In the humanity's eyes, if murder can be considered "sound," what other sins can be regarded as "sound?" Life in such a thoughtless society will consist of alternative lifestyles while having a form of godliness. The philosophical attitude of pragmatism draws away from God's original plan for man.

Accordingly, imagine man as a computer with its hard drive wired according to God's design. As long as the input is God's word, computer/man will function in society in a true form of godliness. If a virus such as critical theory is logged into the computer/man instead of God's word, what would be the cultural sins manifested and observed in this type of society? Computer/man would experience some major difficulties! Society would see apparent evidence of the manifestations of increased violence including brutal murders and suicide, serious sexual perversions, individuals without self-control, proud, arrogant, not lovers of the good, and lovers of pleasure rather than lovers of God (2Tim. 3:16). Man would dabble in the occult world through witchcraft, new age religions, astrology, and sorcery instead of seeking God's scriptural guidance. He would search for curative answers through "holistic techniques" instead of relying upon God's eternal healing. If the spiritual side of man longs for a mystic challenge, he would find it in strange or pseudo religions such as Scientology, Christian Science,

Buddhism, Islam and organizations such as the Free Masons and secret societies.

Manifestations of a superficial society can be categorized into three broad areas, 1) depravation, 2) language, and 3) theology. The first sign is a society embracing a sexual revolution by exhibiting no reins of self control in the areas of homosexuality and lesbianism. Liberty of the carnal heart licenses one to the next level of pedophilia and incest. As humanity seeks pleasure in decadent sins, evil forces will continue to dominate. Chaos results as addressed in scripture, "...God gave them up to a debased mind to do what ought not be done... they not only do them but give approval to those who practice them" (Rom. 1:28-32).

1) **Depravation**. Human sin is certainly not confined to sexual sins but currently we are witnessing a no holds barred mentality in the activities of a depraved world. For instance, LAMBDA (lesbian and man boy defense association) is an organization gaining strength in membership numbers, political clout and legal muscle that advocates gay, lesbian, bisexual, and transgender lifestyles. Its mission as stated on its website, "...to create social change and achieve full civil rights, dignity, and self-respect for gay, lesbian, bisexual, and transgender individuals through education, youth advocacy,

anti-violence efforts, and fighting discrimination of all forms, to achieve full participation in society of persons belonging to a sexual minority." The organization's mission and agenda will be promoted through the current Secretary of Education, a longtime homosexual activist known for his radical education initiatives in the Chicago public school system.

LAMBDA's objectives can easily be met through the president appointed "safe school" czar. (Why a safe school czar when there is a secretary of education? The "safe school" czar operates under Congress' radar). As demonstrated in an article posted in the Washington Times on Monday, September 28, 2008 entitled "'Safe School Czar' Ignored Statutory Rape," the czar failed to protect a fifteen year old boy from having sex with an older man.

In a 2000 speech to a Gay/Lesbian advocacy group that promotes such behaviors in school, the safe school czar stated that he encouraged the relationship between the fifteen year old boy and the older man by emphasizing condom use for the teen. The relationship was also encouraged by the youth's teacher by assuaging any of the youth's concerns so that the teen "left my office with a smile on his face that I would see every time I saw him on the campus for the next two years, until he graduated.'" [97] As the superficial society vies for sexual gratification, sanctity of life is tossed aside as humanity is degraded to an object of pleasure giving.

2) **Language**: One of the main usages needed by CT to breathe new life into its theories is language and words. It hopes to create a superficial language whereby meanings have no intrinsic worth. In this way definitions can be repeated as needed to fit the occasion. Words redressed in new language by wearing new garments as they are stylized in postmodern thinking make one question if there is a new language emerging. The term, "social justice," is a current model that demonstrates a disparity of definitions. Social justice and its plight for the poor is not an altogether bad concept as it originated under the premise of religious meanings. However much to postmodernists' chagrin, whenever taken over by the culprits and reduced to an operational premise that is relative to how it is employed, the true definition is lost.

3) **Liberation Theology**: Similarly in a misguided effort by LT to appeal to the masses and become culturally relevant, the actual Word of God is being sacrificed and massacred in the name of contextualization. Contextualization is the process whereby Biblical passages are interpreted into today's culture. What is happening today as a conse-

quence of Critical theory is "...the attempt to contextualize the Christian faith in terms of contemporary culture [that] produces a syncretic grid that, in our time, in turn gives ultimate priority to our postmodern matrix."[98] When these conditions prevail, Biblical truths and meanings are constructed to reflect the cultural paradigm. Ultimately this allows the window of opportunity to fling open for multiple definitions and the negation of true meanings. When definitions are tampered with, God's Word is being molded around culture instead of culture being molded around God.

From a God-centered culture to a relativistic culture counterfeits of moral ethics and instruction abound to the innocent bystander. In the postmodern world ethics are relegated to a "private sphere" that consists of the confines of the home, family, and individual beliefs. The church will no longer be a beacon of light for humanity but a tiny flicker striving to remain alight. As a pagan polytheism grows in strength and syncretism grips societal structures the question becomes, "Under what conditions will orthodox Christianity be tolerated?" Inevitably in CT's sub culture the future church will appear not so dissimilar to the United Church of Canada. The United Church of Canada may very well exemplify the church in a superficial society.

The United Church of Canada, "...has given up in the Christian sexual ethic of chastity and embraces the promiscuity that says that personal sexual fulfillment trumps social and family duties. It has embraced Western liberal individualism and rejected biblical discipleship. It has removed God's self-revelation in Jesus Christ from the center of church proclamation and inserted a vague spirituality and natural theology in its place. [Religious forms of worship replace the genuine and no evidence of a regeneration occurs in one's life]. Instead of calling people to repentance and faith, the United Church calls them to therapy and self- actualization. Instead of preaching salvation through sin through repentance, it preaches acceptance for every lifestyle. Wherever the secular Canadian culture goes, the United Church will be not far behind; in fact, it will try to be there a bit ahead of the majority culture if at all possible (thus enabling its progressive self-image.) Getting there ten years before the rest of the culture (as on the homosexuality issue) is what passes for being prophetic and progressive in the United Church of Canada today."[99]

The portrait of this Canadian denomination depicts a very shallow, superficial church reminiscent of the value system represented in liberation theology. Will the superficial church equal a superficial society or visa versa? Either way, it's superficial.

In conclusion, an age-old slogan that mirrors the concept of the culprit, Critical Theory is, "All that glitters is not gold!" It describes the state of affairs that exist in the world today because of the misconceptions of truth perpetrated on society by CT's transformation, reshaping, and domination of the world scene. The shiny glitter of CT's concepts of change for the so-called betterment of society catches the eye, but when the dust is blown away the rock is only fool's gold, at best. Copycat, counterfeit nuggets of truth are worth only the nostalgia elicited by a very few philosophers who for the most part were diehard atheist.

The philosophers of CT's grand experiment is leading to a larger scale of change derived from a novel pattern of government that will suffice to bring about a new type of society, economy, and posture towards religion. Increasingly, the convening powers simply expect the people to cave in to the increasing rate of sinful conditions imposed on our civilization. CT's experiment will prove to be a type of hell on earth. Sadly, all of the lawless deeds will eventually surround the righteous just as in the days of Lot in Sodom and Gomorrah. These cities destroyed by God typify the worst of the worst in sinful conditions and rebellion against God. The goal of secular powers of global humanity to tolerate the depravity of man places a cloud of darkness that eventually brings God's wrath (Gen. 6:5).

Most importantly, what happens next? Momentum is building and bigger challenges beckon our immediate attention because the warning signs have been posted. The professing Church as well as the world will come under the great delusion of peace and prosperity by man in the last days (1Thess 5:3).

In order for this setup to take effect, the Christianity of the Bible will be "Out", and the "New and refreshed" Christianity will be "In." The apostate church must appear faithful to Christ, yet it will be so contaminated with hostility toward the true teachings of the Bible as to be unrecognizable to true followers (2 Tim 4:1-4). Noticeably, the true followers of Christ will also be "Out" and the new followers of the apostate religion will be "In." The new Christianity comes packaged so attractively it will easily be accepted by those whose mind-sets have been brainwashed by the false prophets and proponents of Critical Theory thinking. What we are witnessing today is the planned attack on Christianity that is from the forces that emanates from within not totally from external forces. Obviously if the church can be duped, so can the rest of humanity.[100]

Rerun of History. Pre-reformation days witnessed the same ethical corruption we are presently witnessing in today's churches. The early true Christians were despised because they stood against the so called wisdom of the times. Today, the true followers of Jesus Christ are finding themselves in similar conditions. Today's followers of Christ are bombarded with name calling as they hold onto the timeless truths of the Scriptures. In the pre-reformation era, an effort by the Catholic Church to keep its flock docile and the Word of God contained in the Bible was kept from the people. Contemporary liberal Bibles have been proven to take radical steps to keep truth away from the readers. The Catholic Church maintained that the Holy Bible was in the protective hands of the church and should be managed by the priesthood. Such a privilege promoted the intoxicating aura of power, the control of government and religion combined to keep the truth under wraps emerged as corruption in the form of wealth and luxury, money making scheme and power. Absolution of sins was up for sale in the form of indulgences. If one mortally sinned, they could buy an absolution from the church. Not so dissimilar is the present day notion of tithing and financial offerings in order to receive one's blessings. The practice of selling indulgences has passed but the spirit is alive and gaining strength. So also is the Catholic Church's doctrine of works. As is practiced in the Catholic Church if one committed a venial sin, a few "Hail Mary Prayers," a couple of "Act of Contrition Prayers," and a smattering of "Our Father Prayers" thrown in for good measure would satisfy the cost for the venial sin. The things of this life formally and presently did not change over the years as the same corruption still exists.

LT is using the terms peace, social justice, equality, tolerance, spirituality, wholeness, and globalize to return to the former works theology of the pre reformation era. As more and more Roman Catholic practices, rituals, and doctrine are being reintroduced, it will undoubtedly take us back to the apostate church.

Martin Luther, author of the Christian reformation, said with deep concern upon hearing of what was happening in society and the church, "I always expected that Satan would send us this plague." Since those prophetic words were spoken by Luther, contemporary times are reflecting the same infected society and Christianity. Efforts evidenced by the return of the Catholic Church works mentality will push us toward the future to a global society and a global one world religion. (As a matter of fact Catholic means universal. Universal means one.) Universal church means one church, one religion. Whereas global humanism attempts to take the place of the offering of hope of the Holy Spirit, the Holy Spirit's work is the true work that disintegrates the barriers of racial, ethnic, and religious groups; the true global union. Political and social systems derived from humanists, atheists, and Christians working side by side for peace on earth is a biblical impossibility (John 9:40; Rom. 8:1-22). The first inkling of an apostate church deception was mentioned biblically thousands of years ago. Referred to as the "Last Days Church," it incorporates a diabolical scheme to usher in the Anti-Christ. [101]

Liberal theology is closely related to Satan's methodology to exact his deception. When Satan masquerades as the deliverer, and is accepted as the Christ, who must his followers be? One can only deem they must be deceived Christians. In Satan's own beguiling methodology, he will present himself as Christ and intently supplant himself into the churches and society. Christ Jesus announced to the world before his departure that we will see the greatest religious deception of the world in the coming of the last days.

"Look carefully then how you walk, not as unwise but as wise making the best of the time, because the days are evil"

Eph. 5:15-16.

Human perspective would tell us that the evil's roots are profoundly deep; it's gone too far; there's no hope; and no way of turning back. True evil does have deep roots in humanity but that has been the case during many periods of humanity's history. Therefore we must treat each era the same until Christ returns reaching for the lost souls. A godly man named Nehemiah was called by God to restore and rebuild the burned up gates and broken walls of Jerusalem; walls that symbolically represented the hearts and minds of where the people should be in their walk with God. The nation had become easy prey to the enemy because of the sins of worldly pleasure seeking, the lack of self denial and any self sacrifice for Christ's sake. Participants of a worldly society that can be seduced by acquisitiveness of things instead of the things of eternal value will eventually reap the consequences of their selfish decisions. Nehemiah knew his God reigned in sovereignty, wisdom, mercy, grace, and power and that He is a God that can turn the hopelessly rebellious to Himself. Isn't the need close enough to home, your life, your family, friends and nation, yet? Nehemiah 4:14 states, "And I looked, and rose up, and said unto the nobles, and to the rulers, and to the rest of the people, Be not ye afraid of them: remember the Lord, which is great and terrible, and fight for your brethren, your sons, and your daughters, your wives, and your houses."

Babylon was another superficial city and its greatest sin is that she "made all nations drink the wine of the wrath of her fornication." The cup of deception which she offered to the world was filled to the brim with trickery and dishonesty. And as a result of her prostitution the city of Babylon was utterly destroyed. The biblical foreshadowing of why nations fall was given as a road map for future generations to heed for their good. A strong need to re-birth Christianity to its original core doctrine along with a combined effort to reestablish the foundation of the Constitution in America "We the People" should be the cry of all citizens of a strong patriarchal society.

Each time God has intervened on behalf of the people He has used a prophet or person to bring the message. Nehemiah's vision to save the culture was nonetheless a daunting and debasing job but he was called, motivated, determined, and fearless. Obviously, a man who knew what his God could and would do stated, "Then answered I them, and said unto them, The God of heaven, he will prosper us; <u>therefore we his servants will arise and build...</u>" (Neh. 2:20). May we all be blessed with the spirit of Nehemiah, his passion and courage, to fight and rebuild concurrently passing the torch to the next generation so that unbeknownst to them they will not walk in a superficial society! If you build they will come.....

APPENDIX 1

BIBLE STUDY
CHRISTIAN SOCIALISM –
TRUE OR FALSE
– Acts 2-4; Matthew 20: 1-15

S trangely, CT's claims have set in motion a way of looking at Scripture that have been captured by the pseudo-intellectuals and from their perspective the assessment is that certain scriptures promote socialism. In a word, liberal thinkers who believe that wealth distribution and economic leveling is the example, set forth biblically, for the government to propose for the people to follow. No doubt, religious social ethic has and always will have a concern for the poor. Therefore, there are a few factors to be settled before coming to a succinct decision if scriptures were intended to promote the Marxist concept of socialism.

During different time periods of history the appearance was that "industrial capitalism" was unfair. Leaders of this type of capitalism seemed unconcerned with the welfare of its employers; therefore reformers and progressives began an incline toward bigger government for the rights of labor and other socialist concepts. The burden of poverty was so dire during these times that the opportunity arose for the government to form a type of brotherhood of service to individuals that served the government without promotion or evangelizing the people for God.

Today, we are witnessing this social gospel played out by big government and liberal politicians as well as liberal theologians. One of the methods used to accomplish the agenda is done by manipulating the Scriptures starting with the book of Acts. Many liberal theologians are suggesting that the book of Acts mirrors the philosophy of socialistic principles. With this type of thinking the question becomes: When the early church began, did the following Scriptures set a pattern that demonstrates the basis for "Christian Socialism?" (Acts 2:45, 4:32-35, 5:11)

And the multitude of them that believed were of one heart
and of one soul: neither said any of them that ought of

the things which he possessed was his own: but they had
all things Jesus; and great grace was upon them all [34]
Neither was there any among them that lacked; for as
many as were possessors of lands or houses sold them, and
brought the process of the things that were sold, [35] And
laid them down at the apostles' feet; and distribution was
made unto every man according as he
had need (Acts 4:32-35).

The strength of these Scriptures lies in the Greek word, "*koinonia* – (fellowship)." *Koinonia* means "commonness" or "commonality" a word that denotes a kind of sharing something with someone, contributing, or giving. The point being that the church (believers) through the spirit of God commonly cared for and had deep concern for other believers. Basically it was a supernatural type of brotherly love.

The grace of the Lord Jesus Christ, and the love of God,
and the communion of the Holy Ghost,
be with you all. Amen.
(2 Cor. 13:14)

So, how is the social gospel concept possible for all the people, all the time, when the whole of the book of Acts was founded and organized by a community of believers of faith in the risen Christ and by the power of the Holy Spirit? Are progressives and liberals attempting to use biblical concepts for their answers to society's ills? Certainly worldly concepts have never wanted to give validity to Scripture before and certainly even if they did, it could only produce a counterfeit concept/false religion without the supernatural power of the Holy Spirit.

Clearly in the early church communal distribution was a description of those who are in Christ *(not of the world)*. Commonly they had invoked a decision on their own recognizance to share everything due to the fact that at this time in the first century, the economic emergency in Jerusalem was dire. The very first Christians were Jews who had attempted to continue going to the synagogue to worship. Other Jews were rejecting and ostracizing the believers for believing, Jesus was the Messiah, an affront to the religious zealots of the day. Ultimately, the believers had to break from their Jewish roots resorting to house gatherings in order to worship Jesus leaving them without the common resources of the land. According to all historical accounts no evidence exist that communal distribution was practiced in other churches of the Empire (Acts 11:27-30, 1 Cor. 16:2, 2 Cor.8:11, 9, 6-11, 1 Tim.6:17-19). The Word goes on to say that donations had to be taken and were offered freely from other churches to help fund the Jerusalem communal church because the need was so dire (Rom. 15:25-31, 1 Cor.16:1-3, Gal.2:10).

Viewing these events in Scripture shows that the social-istic concept of communal distribution was not a mandate or pattern from God or the ruling government; it was a des-perate decision that was made amongst the people of God for each other's well being. Mainly what the Scripture offers to our understanding is the, *"Koinonia* spirit" –an attitude within the church itself to embrace conviction of the Holy Spirit to have an unselfish heart attitude toward the poor and needy. Voluntarily, the Jerusalem believers sold pieces of their property as needed to help their brother and sister; thereby demonstrating brotherly love by sharing unity and generosity. For the Christian, what the Old Testament dem-onstrates is the actions of the people at work in the human affairs of those in need (Deut. 15:1-3, 7-11,13-14, Lev. 19:10, 23:22).

Furthermore, for those who believe the following Scripture concerning Ananias and Sapphira confirm their findings of wealth distribution, let's look (Acts 5:1-11). Reading carefully you realize the reason they were struck down was the sin of dishonesty and lying to the people of God and the Holy Spirit. Scripture shows that they had their own choice as to whether to sell the land and give as much as they desired, not a demand by anyone. Unfortunately, they decided to make themselves appear more magnanimous than they were, lying cost them everything.

Due to the fact that there were no capitalist's institutions until the turn of the 17th century, how could the Jerusalem followers have based their decisions on fighting the existing capitalist system? Wealth distribution and taxing by demand, due to the state law, is a far cry than freely sacrificially and benevolently giving to the poor. Favoritism toward the rich or the poor illustrates the breaking of God's law as stated in the book of James 2:29:

> *"But if ye have respect to persons, ye commit sin, and are convinced of the law as transgressors."*

Does Matthew 20:1-5 Advocate Socialism?

Former national chairman of the socialist party, Norman Thomas, used the parable in Matthew 20:1-15 to justify socialism! In the Scripture immediately following (20:16) Christ related to the fact, *"But many that are first shall be last; and the last shall be first."* This happens right after the parable *(a moral or religious lesson that may be learned)* of the workers being paid equally. But is any part of this parable meant to defend our use of a monetary value system or is it meant to describe God's grace, goodness, and salvation? You decide!

"These last men have worked only one hour, and you made them equal to us who have borne the burden and the heat of the day." (Matt. 20:12)
"Is your eye envious because I am generous?"
(Matt. 20:15, NAS)

How can socialism be when consistently these principles when used in the world system have proven to bring a tyrannical system producing totalitarian governments? What's wrong? A system using Godly principles without the assistance of the Holy Spirit can and never will produce anything good. Man without the supernatural intervention of God can never produce the virtues of the biblical calling, evil ways will persistently prevail.

To confuse these passages with the concept of socialistic wealth distribution or money in any way destroys the beauty of its meaning. What is clear is the demonstration of evil mans' jealousy and envy corrupting their thinking and questioning God's sovereignty. No one deserves eternal life-salvation. At times it is hard to understand that the person who has come to Christ at the last moments of life (Luke 23:40-43), or after doing things so vile that that he could be given the same grace as those who have all their lives served Christ and His sayings. But as shown in the parable of the vineyard owner who is representative of God, He is speaking to religious believers who are new in the Kingdom as well as those who have spent tremendous time with Christ (Matt.20: 1-16). He is embracing the thought that it's not about how long or deserving you may feel, but about God's grace and mercy. In God's kingdom membership is not about who has the most money – rules, or a position or title.

In the previous parable in the Bible of the rich young man, Jesus tells the rich young man to sell all his possession and give his money to the poor (Matt.19:16-20). Why? Was Christ promoting socialism? Rather this story was about having money as an idol. The love of money (a graven image) was the moral of the story thereby disgracing the first commandments, "there will be not other gods before me" (Exodus 20:3). Christ knew the ugliness in this man's heart and He confronted him where it hurts, his wallet. With this the man tucked tail and ran for he was not willing to part with his money in any way. Christ had asked him to give up his idol, to change this one thing hindering his character from receiving eternal salvation. How can the temple of God be in agreement with idol (1Cor. 3:16, 2 Cor. 6:16)?

Do not lay up for yourselves treasures on earth, where moth and rust destroy, and where thieves break in and steal, but lay up for yourselves treasures in heaven, where neither moth nor rust destroy, and where thieves do not break in and steal. For where your treasure is, there will your heart will be also (Matt. 6:19-21).

The carnal explorers of CT's combination of a postmodern socialist movement will attempt to deceive Christians with the humane concepts of goodness, love, and community. All these words ring bells in the Christian's ear; nonetheless, this is self-enlightenment that leads to the redefinition of man, without the incarnation or the story of the atoning work of righteousness or the born again experience of Christianity. In other words, salvation is being reinterpreted to mean social and political action, by works, rather than faith through Jesus Christ. With CT, absolute truths will become more extinct than pre-historic dinosaurs. God will no longer be in charge of you as an individual orchestrating His life plan (Psalm 139:13-16). Instead the government and the anti-Christ spirit will rule and reign.

A CHRISTIAN'S DUTY TO CIVIL GOVERNMENT – Romans 13

W e can all identify with the feelings of frustration toward the submission to unrighteous policies and philosophies, especially the disobedience to God's biblical principles (Acts 4: 18; 5: 17-29). Within God's original plan, our civil government was established as a watchdog against oppression, hostility, and threats for all of society's welfare and against all heathen type of religious influence from individuals or nations (Romans 13). The government was to be a defender of the moral and ethical laws of the land (Romans 13:3). Does government have the right to maintain strict control of our individual freedom? What is the Christian's line of defense against government?

A strong reason exists for the limitation of government rule. If the government rest in the hands of unregenerate men the likelihood of evil persist (Romans 13). What if he is the wrong doer, an agent for evil, not good? Are we still to obey and bow down to evil? If these laws call for you to violate moral and ethical standards established by the word of God, how are we to handle the situation? Yes, we are still required to obey the righteous laws of the land but there are ways to legally and justifiably counter evil thoughts of the government and against the justice system, by voting, and participating in peaceful rallies. We are still called to be responsible citizens who fight for the righteousness that has been established in the Word.

Just as the disciples were threatened, beaten, jailed, tortured and executed for the convictions, we are to walk in their shoes. Yes, standing up for righteousness has consequences, but we are called to stand.

All that is necessary for the triumph of evil is that good men do nothing
-Edmund Burke

Generally, reformations have been the backbone of Christian freedom, standing up for truth from tyrannical powers that be for many centuries. The English theologian, John Wycliffe (1320-1384), translator of the first manuscript for the lay person, The English New Testament, took on Roman powers and Church reform insisting that Christ-not the Pope-was the Head of the Church, and the Bible-not the Catholic Church-was the sole authority for the believer. He was charged with, blasphemy, scandal, pride and heresy. He paid the price![102] It has been said, "The martyr's blood became the seed that would reproduce for centuries to come."

Bonhoeffer asks, "Who stands fast? Only the man whose final standard is not his reason, his principles, his conscience, his freedom or his virtue, but who is ready to sacrifice all this when he is called to obedient and responsible action in faith and in exclusive allegiance to God; The responsible man, who tries to make his whole life an answer to the question and call of God. Where are the responsible people?" [103]

Persecution because of standing up for classical ortho-doxy has and always will be part of the cost of being a disciple of Christ. Just recently, you may have read the story of the modern day martyrs for Christ. Three Pastors were recently beheaded by Islamic radicals because of an insurgence of Islamic religion sweeping across their area. They were told to accept Islam or die, a statement not so far from our backdoor. They chose death.

APPENDIX 3

BIBLICAL ECONOMICS "101"

President Roosevelt stated, "The lesson of history confirmed by the evidence immediately before me, show conclusively that continued dependence upon relief induces a spiritual and moral disintegration fundamental destructive to the national fiber. To dole out relief in this way is to administer a narcotic, a subtle destroyer of the human spirit... Rich and the poor become equally poor."

The American way of free enterprise based on solid biblical principles is more closely relational to biblical standards. Free enterprise is demonstrated all throughout the Bible by the buying and selling of goods for profit (free enterprise), whereby you prosper if what you have produced is good and suffer personal consequences if failure occurs.

Promotion happens on the job if you have done well and dismissal takes place if you don't. Considering this method basically everyone is an independent contractor of some sort even if you work for someone else. You perform a service and receive payment.

The epistles, the 21 letters written to the churches in the New Testament, set forth fundamental principles applicable to the structure of the church. Paul's directions laid out to the Thessalonian Church is directive of the principle for all churches as stated in 2 Thessalonians 3: 10-12, "For even when we were with you, we would give you command; if any is not willing to work, let him not eat. [11] For we hear that some among you walk in idleness, not busy at work, but busybodies. [12] Now such persons we command and encourage in the Lord Jesus Christ to do their work quietly and to earn their own living."

The prototype of socialism found in Europe where the socialist mindset has taken root is presently dying. It shows that primarily there is little incentive to work hard because government benefits costs too much money to maintain. As a consequence there is massive taxation and reason not to work hard. Workers are guaranteed a certain standard of living and entitlement to services, but the more you work, the more you pay in taxes. Little opportunity exists for an ambitious person with a great idea for entrepreneurship to succeed in Europe. Contrast that with the U.S.A. in which immigrants risk life and limb to come here to work and have an opportunity to better oneself because of the free enterprise system (although as of late, we wonder if this still holds true as many immigrants are returning home.) Nevertheless, people considered in poverty in this country are better off than their counterparts in other countries. Socialism is all about becoming self-sufficient, good enough in your own flesh as to create a world without the all sufficient God (Jehovah-Jireh- Gen. 22). The capitalist system may not be perfect, it certainly has flaws, but it allows God to be God. It means that our dependence upon daily living and our daily bread should be upon God, not government (Matt. 6:25-34, 1Tim. 6:6-10); otherwise who becomes your god?

BIBLIOGRAPHY

Bennett, William. *The Book of Virtue*. New York: Simon and Schuster, 1993.

Bullock, Allan. *Hitler: A Study of Tyranny*. San Francisco: HarpersOne, 1991.

Carter, Craig. *Rethinking Christ and Culture. A Post-Christiandom Perspective*. Grand Rapids: Brazoo Press, 2006.

Carson, D. A. *The Gagging of God*. Grand Rapids: Zondervan, 2004.

Castells, Manuel. "Afterward: Why Networks Matter?" in *Network Logic: Who Governs in an Interconnected World*, edited by M. Helen, P. Miller, and P. Skidmore. London: Demos, 2004.

Cobley, Paul and Litza Jansz. *Introducing Semiotics.* Cambridge: Icon Books, 2007.

Colson, Chuck. *Chuck Colson Speaks,* Promise Press, 2000.

Coulter, Ann. *Godless.* New York: Crown Forum, 2006.

Driscoll, Mark. *Confessions of a Reformission Rev.: Hard Lessons from an Emerging Missional Church.* Grand Rapids: Zondervan, 2006.

Dubiel, Helmut. "The origins of Critical Theory: An Interview with Leo Lowenthal" in *Telos* 14, no. 3, (1981): 141-54.

Durant, Will. *The Story of Philosophy.* New York: Washington Square Press, 1961.

Egar, Joseph, *Einstein's Violin.* New York: Penguin Group, 2005.

Eidsmoe John. *God and Caesar.* Wheaton: Crossway Books, 1984.

Feinberg, Andrew and William Leiss, eds. *The Essential Marcuse. Selected Writings of Philosopher and*

Social Critic Herbert Marcuse. Boston: Beacon Press, 2007.

Gregor, Brian and Jens Zimmerman, eds. *Bonhoeffer and Continental Thought*. Indianapolis: Indiana University Press, 2009.

Grudem, Wayne. *Systematic Theology*. Grand Rapids: Zondervan, 1994.

Hank Hanegraaff *Christianity in Crisis,* Eugene: Harvest House Publishers, 1997

Hart, Archibald. *Thrilled to Death*. Nashville: Thomas Nelson, 2007.

Hughes, Kent, R. *Acts. The Church Afire*. Wheaton: Crossway Books, 1996.

Hunt, Dave. *The Archon Conspiracy*. Eugene: Harvest House, 1989.

Hunt, Dave and T. A. McMahon. *The Seduction of Christianity*. Eugene: Harvest House, 1985.

Inspirational Christian Library. *The Timeless Writings of C. S. Lewis*. New York: Inspirational Press, 1981.

Johnson, Gary, L. W. and Ronald N. Gleason, eds. *Reforming or Conforming? Post-Conservative Evangelicals and the Emerging Church*. Wheaton: Crossway Books, 2008.

Keller, Timothy. *The Reason for God*. New York: Penquin Group, 2008.

Kennedy, James, D. *The Gates of Hell Shall Not Prevail*. Nashville: Thomas Nelson, 1996.

Jones, Deanna Blackmon. *The Faith Arena*. Xulon Press, 2007

Lewis, C. S. *The Abolition of Man*. New York: Macmillan, 1975.

Lutzer, Erwin W. *Who Are You to Judge*. Chicago: Moody Publishers, 2002.

MacArthur, John F. *In the Footsteps of Faith*. Wheaton: Crossway Books, 1998.

Marcuse, Herbert. *Eros and Civilization*. Boston: Beacon, 1955.

Martinich A. P. *Philosophical Writing* Malden: Blackwell Publishers, 1998.

McLaren, Brian. *A Generous Orthodoxy.* Grand Rapids: Zondervan, 2004.

_____. A New Kind of Christian. *A Tale of Two Friends on a Spiritual Journey.* San Francisco: Jossey-Bass, 2001.

McDowell, Josh and Bob Hostetler. *Right From Wrong.* Nashville: Thomas Nelson, 1994.

Morris, Dick. *Fleeced.* New York: Harper Collins, 2008.

Naremore James and Patrick Brantlinger. *Modernity and Mass Culture.*Indianapolis: Indiana University Press, 1991.

O'Reilly, Bill. *Culture Warrior.* New York: Broadway Books, 2006.

Pagitt, Doug. *Reimaging Spiritual Formation: A Week in the Life of an Experimental Church.* Grand Rapids: Zondervan, 2004.

Pfeiffer, Charles F., Howard F.Vos and John Rea. *Wycliffe Bible Dictionary*. Hendrickson Pub., 1975.

Piper, John and Justin Taylor, *The Supremacy of Christ in a Postmodern World*. Wheaton: Crossway Books, 2007, http://cdn.desiringgod.org/pdf/books_bcpw/books_bcpw.pdf

Preston, Ronald H. *Confusions in Christian Social Ethics*. Grand Rapids: Eerdmans Publishers, 1994.

Quin, Sherrer and Ruthanne Garlock. *A Women's Guide to Breaking Bondages*. Ann Arbor: Servant Publishers, 1994.

Schweppenhouser, Gerhard. Translated by James Rolleston. *Theodor Adorno. An Introduction*. Durham: Duke University Press, 2009.

Sims, Stuart and Borin Van Boon. *Introduction to Critical Theory, A Graphic Guide*. London: Icon Books, 2009.

Smalley, Gary and John Trent, Ph.D. T*he Language of Love*. Focus on the Family Pub. 1991.

Sproul, R. C. *The Consequences of Ideas. Understanding the Concepts That Shaped Our World.* Wheaton: Crossway Books, 2000.

_____. T*he Mystery of the Holy Spirit.* Carol Stream: Tyndale House. 1990.

_____.*Surprised by Suffering.* Carol Stream: Tyndale House. 1988.

_____. *Reason to Believe.* Grand Rapids: Zondervan, 1982.

Webber, Robert, E. *Ancient-Future Faith. Rethinking Evangelicalism for a Postmodern World.* Grand Rapids: Baker Books, 1999.

_____. *Listening in the Beliefs of Emerging Churches: Five Perspectives.* Grand Rapids: Zondervan, 2007.

Wells, David. *The Courage to be Protestant.* Grand Rapids: Eerdsman Publishing Co., 2008.

White, E. G. *America in Prophecy.* Jamison: Inspiration Books East, Inc. 1988.

ELECTRONIC BIBLIOGRAPHY

Armstrong, Chris, "The Futrue Lies in the Past," http://www. christianitytoday.com/ct/2008/february/22.22.html

Ayleswoth, Gayle, "Postmodernism," http://plato.standford. edu.entries/postmoderism/

Biblical Discernment Ministries, "Robert Schuller. General Teachings/ Activities," http://www.rapidnet. com/~jbeard/bdm/exposes/schuller/general.htm

"Bill Ayres" www.DiscoverTheNetwork.org

Billy Graham Center, "The Chicago Call-Collection 33," http://www.wheaton.edu/bgc/archives/ GUIDES/033.htm

Blunden, Andy, "The Culture Industry: Enlightenment as Mass Deception," http://www.marxists.org/reference/archive/adorno/1944/culture-industry

Calderone, Michael's Blog: Sen. Stabenow Wants Hearings on Radio 'Accountability;' Fairness Doctrine," http://www.politico.com/blogs/michaelcalderone/0209/sen_stabenow_wants_hearings_on_radio_accountability_talks_fairness_doctrine.html?

Craven, Michael, "Apologetics in the 21st Cent.-part v," http://www.crosswalk.com/news/11601563?

Editorial in Washington Post 9-28-09 "'Safe School' Czar Ignored Statutory Rape," http://www.sweetness-light.com/archive/safe-school-czar-ignored-statutory-rape

Enotes: "Theodor Adorno 1903-1969," http://www.enotes.com?twentieth-century-criticism/adorno-theodor

Farr, Arnold, "Critical Theory." http://www/aspect.vt.edu/papers/Farr/CriticalTheory

The Federal Web Manager Council, "Putting Citizens First: Transforming Online Government," http://www.

usa.gov/webcontent/documents/Federal_Web_
Manager_WhitePaper.pdf

Friedeburg, Ludwig, "History of the Institute of Social
Research (Summary)," http://www.ifs.uni-frankfurt.
de/english/history.htm

"The Frankfurt School and Critical Theory," http://www.
marxists.org/subject/frankfurt-school/index.htm

Garland, Christian, "Adorno: Negation as Theory and
Method," http://www.gseis.ucla.edu/faculty/kellner

Harvard Educational Review, "Lesbian, Gay, Bisexual and
Transgender People and Education," http://www.
gse.harvard.edu/~hepg/sum96.html

Hammer, Rhonda and Douglas Kellner, "Third Wave
Feminism, Sexualities, and the Adventure of the
Posts," http://gseis.ucla.edu/faculty/kellner/html

Hammond, Peter, "The Greatest Killer," http://www.christian.
org.za/firearmsnews/2004-04_the greatestkiller.htm

"Hegelian Dialect and Conspiracy," http://www.
biblebelievers.biz/bb970219.htm

Kappelman, Todd, "Dietrich Bonhoeffer," http://www. leaderu.com/orgs/probe/docs/bonhoeffer.html

Kellner, Douglas, "Critical Perspectives on Television From the Frankfurt School to Postmodernism," http://www.gseis.ucla.edu/faculty/kellner/

_____,"Critical Theory and the Crisis of Social Theory," http://www.gseis.ucla.edu/faculty/kellner/kellner.html

_____, "Toward a Critical Theory of Education," http:// gseis,ucla.edu/faculty/kellner/

"Kelos vs. New London, Ct.," www.law.cornell.edu/supct/ html/04-108.ZS.html

Kruger, M. J. "The Sufficiency of Scripture in Apologetics," http://www.tms.edu.tmsj/tmsj12m.pdf

Litvak, Anya, "Estate Taxes:Fate of Bush's Inheritance Tax Phaseout Plan Remains Unclear," http://www. bizjournals.com/pittsburgh/stories/2010/04/26/ focusl.html

Mahon, T. A. "Ancient-Future Heresies," http://www. thebereancall.org/node/6535

Morrisey, Ed, "Pew:Unions Approval Rating Plummets,"
http://www.hotair.com/archives/2010/02/24/
pew-approval-ratings-plummets/

Noyes, Rich, "Barack Obama and Bill Ayres, Stanley Kurtz
Makes the Connection," http://www.newsbuster.
org/blog/rich-noyes/2008/09/23/barack-obama-bill-
ayres-stanley-kurtz-makes-connection

O'Kelly, Brendan, "Delueze and Guattari: A Thousand
Plateaus," http://www.colorado.edu/English/
courses/klages/2010/2brendan.html

Osteen, Philip, "Critical theory, the Frankfurt School and
the Use of 'Negation' to Identify Trandscendental
Possibilities: Horkheimer, Adorno, and
Marcuse," http://www.portfolio.du.edu/portfolio/
getportfoliofile?uid=19187

Pearce, David, "The Hedonistic Imperative,"
http://www.hedweb.com
http://www.radicalteaching.org

"Railway Industry Overview Series-Government Regulatory Requirements-October 2007" www.irs. gov/businesses/article/0,,id=175295,00.html

"Raising Resident Aliens" www.baylor.edu/content/ services/document.php/87233.pdf

Robinson, Daniel, N. "The Great Ideas of Philosophy, 2nd ed." Course No. 4200. http://www. shareseeking.com/Great-Ideas-of-Philosophy-2nd-Edition_439832.html

Rowen, John, "John Rowen: Dialectical Thinking" http:// www.gwiep.net

Rogers, Everett, M., "The Critical School and Consumer Research," http://www.acrwebsite.org/volumes/ display.asp?id=6624

Sherk, James, "EFCA Authorizes Gov't Control of 4 Million Small Businesses," http://www.heritage.org/ research?reports/2009/03/EFCA-Authorizes-Gov't-Control-of-4-Million-Small-Business

Solomon, Robert. "No Excuses: Existentialism and the Meaning of Life" Course No. 437. http://www.

heroturko.org/tutorials/other-tutorials/92751-no-excuses-existentialism-and-the-meaning-of-life.html

Troyes, Nancy and Binjamin Appelbaum, "Government Crack Down on Unfair Credit Card Practices." www.washingtonpost.com/wpdyn/content/story/2008/12/18/ST20088121801947.html

Worts, Phil, "Community (Communist) Oriented Policy," http://www.newswithviews.com/community_policy_/community_policy.htm

Endnotes

[1] C. S. Lewis, *The Abolition of Man* (New York: Macmillan, 1975), pp. 56-7.

[2] Daniel N. Robinson, Distinguished Professor Emeritus Oxford University and Georgetown University, *The Great Ideas of Philosophy, 2nd Edition*, Course No. 4200.

[3] R. C. Sproul, *The Consequences of Ideas. Understanding the Concepts that Shaped Our World* (Wheaton: Crossway Books, 2000).

[4] Robert Solomon, Professor of Business and Philosophy, The University of Texas at Austin, *No Excuses: Existentialism and the Meaning of Life*. Course No. 437.

[5]Michael Craven, *Apologetics in the 21ˢᵗ Century – part V,* http://www.crosswalk.com/news/11601563/ Relativism is defined as a differing according to circumstances, persons, cultures.

[6] Philosophy – the search for knowledge and wisdom henceforth leading to the doubt of one's cherished beliefs, dogmas, and axioms.

[7] Propaganda – effort directed towards the advancement of an opinion or plan of action by gaining public support.

[8] Social Justice: -"... generally refers to the idea of creating an egalitarian society or institution that is based on the principles of equality and solidarity, that understands and values human rights, and that recognizes the dignity of every human being. It is part of a Catholic social teaching based on the work of work of St. Thomas Aquinas, and adopted by the Jesuit Luigi Taparelli in the 1840's. Some tenets of social justice have been adopted by those on the left of the political spectrum. They base it on the concepts of human rights and equality and involves a greater degree of economic egalitarianism through progressive taxation, income redistri-

bution, or even property redistribution. Social Justice sometimes 'Social Equality and Global Equality and Economic is Justice – Social and Global Equality or Economic Justice.' The Canadian party (Green Party) define the principle as the 'equitable distribution of resources to ensure that all have full opportunities for personal and social development' Social Justice was also the name of a periodical published by Father Coughlin in the 1930's and early 1940's. He termed 'the Christian principles of social justice' as an alternative to both capitalism and communism. But the catholic radical alliance felt that he misused the term and was supportive of capitalism." Wikipedia, the free encyclopedia; http://en.wikipedia.org/wiki/social justice

[9] Communism is defined as any social system that calls for abolition of private property and control of society for the common use over economic profit. Socialism is public ownership and control of production, distribution, and exchange of materials assuring each member of society an equal share of goods, services, and welfare benefits.

[10] Peter Hammond, "The Greatest Killer," http://www.christianaction.org.za/firearmnews/2004-04_thegreatestkiller.htm

[11] Utopia was originally coined by Sir Thomas More in 1516 when he wrote about an imaginary island with a perfect political and social system.

[12] Allan Bullock, *Hitler: A Study of Tyranny* (San Francisco: Harpers One, 1991), 399.

[13] Brian Gregor and Jens Zimmermann, eds., *Bonhoeffer and Continental Thought* (Indianapolis: Indiana University Press, 2009), 90.

[14] William J. Bennett, *The Book of Virtue* (New York: Simon and Schuster, 1993), 599.

[15] Brian Gregor and Jens Zimmerman, eds., *Bonhoeffer and Continental Thought* (Indianapolis: Indiana University Press, 2009), 8.

[16]Max Horkheimer - The Father of Critical Theory was born in Stuttgard, Germany to a wealthy Jewish family. He was educated at the Munch University in Frankfurt where he met Theodor Adorno. He emigrated to America in 1954 and until 1959 he lectured at the University of Chicago. Horkheimer

developed Critical Theory through a mix of radical and conservative lenses that stem from radical Marxism and ending in "pessimistic Jewish transcendentalism. After his immigration to the United States, he accepted an offer from Columbia University in New York for the Frankfurt Institute to relocate. Theodor Adorno and he wrote "Dialectic Enlightenment" which is about current social mindsets and effects on individuals. The book states that current social mindsets are a result of ideological indoctrination and as such it is a means to quell any form of expression that might contest the given paradigm of thinking. After returning to Europe he became a professor at the University of Frankfurt and focused on reestablishing the Institute there. Eventually he became the first director of the Institute and continued to serve as a regular visiting professor at the University of Chicago. www.plato.stanford.edu

[17] Andrew Feinberg and William Leiss, eds., *The Essential Marcuse. Selected Writings of Philosopher and Social Critic Herbert Marcuse* (Boston: Beacon Press, 2007), xx.

[18]"Marcuse gained notoriety in the United States as a philosopher, social, and political theorist. During the 1960's and

1970's he became one of the most influential intellectuals in the United States. In 1934, he fled from Nazism and emigrated to the United States where he lived most of his life. He worked at the Institute of Social Research and was granted offices and academic affiliation with Columbia University. His first major work in English, 'Reason and Revolution', 1941, traced the ideas of Hegel, Marx and modern social theory. He introduced many English readers to Hegelian-Marxian tradition of dialectical thinking. In 1941, Marcuse joined the OSS (Office of Secret Services) and then worked in the state department becoming the head of the Central European Bureau serving in the U.S government from 1941-the early 1950's. In 1958 he had a tenured position at Brandies University. In 1964 he published 'One-Dimensional Man' a wide ranging critique of both advanced capitalist and communist societies. The text theorized the decline of revolutionary potential in capitalist societies and the development of new forms of social control. This book was followed by a series of books and articles which articulated new left politics." Documented by Professor Douglas Kellner, a modern disciple of Marcuse. You can contact him at the University of California, L.A. He is in the social science and comparative education department. kellner@ucla.edu

[19] Imperialism – a state of domination commonly viewed as in national policies developed to extend one's influence in other countries.

[20] A. P. Martinich, *Philosophical Writing* (Malden: Blackwell Publishers, 1998), 138.

[21] Andrew Feinberg and William Leiss, eds., *The Essential Marcuse. Selected Writings of Philosophy and Social Critic Herbert Marcuse* (Boston: Beacon Press 2007), xxix-xxx.

[22] Ibid.

[23] Niki Raapana and Nordica Friedrich, "What is the Hegelian Dialectic," http://www.crossroad.to/articles2/05/dialectic.htm

[24] Hegemony - Marxist philosopher, Antonio Gramsci, originated the term as the dominance of one social group over another. In a culturally diverse society, a social group can

be ruled and dominated by one of its social classes. http://en.wikipedia.org/wiki/cultural

[25] Brian McLaren, *A New Kind of Christian. A Tale of Two Friends on a Spiritual Journey* (San Francisco: Jossey-Bass, 2001), 100.

[26] Everett M. Rogers, "The Critical School and Consumer Research," http://www.acrwebsite.org/volumes/display.asp?id=6624

[27] Phil Worts, "Community (Communist) Oriented Policing, http://www.newswithviews.com/community_policing/community_ policing.htm

[28] Josh McDowell, *Right From Wrong* (Nashville: Thomas Nelson, 1994), 60.

[29] Archibald Hart, *Thrilled to Death* (Nashville: Thomas Nelson, 2007).

[30]See *Radical Teacher. A Socialist, Feminist, and Anti-Racial Journal on the Theory and Practice of Teaching*, a tri-annual

publication by the University of Illinois Press, 1325 South Oak Street, Champaign, IL 61820. http://www.radicalteaching.org

[31] Will Durant, *The Story of Philosophy* (New York: Washington Square Press, 1961), 401.

[32] Rich Noyes, "Barack Obama and Bill Ayres, Stanly Kurtz Makes the Connection," http://www.newsbusters.org/blog/rich-noyes/2008/09/23/barack-obama-bill-ayres-stanley-kurtz-makes-connection

[33] Rhonda Hammer and Douglas Kellner, "Third Wave Feminism, Sexualities, and the Adventure of the Posts," http://gseis.ucla.edu/faculty/kellner/kellner.html

[34] David Pearce, "The Hedonistic Imperative," www.hedweb.com

[35] Paul Cobley and Litza Jansz, *Introducing Semiotics* (Cambridge: Icon Books, 2007).

[36] Joseph Eger, *Einstein's Violin* (New York: Penguin Group, 2005), 369.

[37] The presidential inaugural address in the *New York Times*, January 21, 1961.

[38] Kelo vs. New London, Connecticut.

[39] Nancy Trejos and Binyamin Appelbaum, "Government Crack Down on Unfair Credit Card Practices," http://www.washingtonpost.com/wp-dyn/content/story/2008/12/18/ST2008121801947.html

[40] Anya Litvak "Estate Taxes: Fate of Bush's Inheritance Tax Phaseout Plan Remains Unclear," http://www.bizjournal.com/pittsbur/stories/2010/04/26/focus1.html

[41] James Sherk, "EFCA Authorizes Government Control of Four Million Small Businesses," http://www.heritage.org/Research?Reports/2009/03/EFCA-Authorzes-Government-Control-of-4-Million-Small-Businesses

[42] Michael Calderone's Blog: Sen. Stabenow Wants Hearings On Radio 'Accountability;' Fairness Doctrine, http://www.politico.com/blogs/michaelcalderone/0209/sen_stabenow_wants_hearings_on_radio_accountability_talks_fairness_doctrine.html?

[43] The Federal Web Managers Council, "Putting Citizens First: Transforming Online Government," http://www.usa.gov/webcontent/documents/Federal_ Web_Managers_ WhitePaper.pdf

[44] Railway Industry Overview Series-Government Regulatory Requirements- October, 2007, http:// www.irs.gov/businesses/article/0,,id=175295,00.html

[45] Ed Morrisey, "Pew: Unions Approval Rating Plummets," http://hotair.com/archives/2010/02/24/pew-unions-approval-rating-plummets/

[46]Brendan O'Kelly, "Deleuze and Guattari," http://colorado.edu/English/courses/klages/2010/2brendan.html

[47]Manuel Castells "Afterward: Why Networks Matter?" in *Network Logic: Who Governs in an Interconnected World,* eds. M. Helen, P. Miller and P. Skidmore (London: Demos, 2004), 224.

[48]Brendan O'Kelly, "Deleuze and Guattari," http://colorado.edu/English/courses/klages/2010/2brendan.html

[49]Herbert Marcuse, *Eros and Civilization* (Boston: Beacon, 1955), 97.

[50]Liberation theology has been described by proponents as "an interpretation of Christian faith through the poor's suffering, their struggle and hope, and a critique of society and the Catholic faith and Christianity through the eyes of the poor", and by detractors as Christianity perverted by Marxism and Communism. http:/en.wikipedia.org/wiki/social justice

[51] Quin Sherrer and Ruthane Garlock, *A Woman's Guide to Breaking Bondages* (Ann Arbor: Servant Publishers, 1994), 162.

[52] Liberation theology: an international and inter-denominational movement within the Catholic Church in Latin

America in the 1950's – 1960's and achieving prominence in the 1970's and 1980's. The term was coined by the Peruvian priest Gustavo Gutierrez who wrote one of the movement's most famous books, *A Theology of Liberation* (1971). Social Justice was also the name of a periodical published by Father Coughlin in the 1930's and early 1940's. Coughlin made a series of broadcasts in which he outlined what he termed "the Christian principles of social justice" as an alternative to both capitalism and communism. Some Catholic contemporaries, such as the Catholic Radical Alliance, felt that he misused the term, and was too supportive of capitalism. http:/en.wikipedia.org/wiki/social justice

[53] Liberation theology: http://www.gotquestions.org/liberation- theology.html

[54] D. A. Carson, *The Gagging of God* (Grand Rapids: Zondervan, 1996), 19.

[55] Brian McLaren, *A Generous Orthodoxy* (Grand Rapids: Zondervan, 2004), 260,262,264.

[56] Timothy Keller, "The Gospel and the Supremacy of Christ in a Postmodern World" in *The Supremacy of Christ in a Postmodern World*, eds. John Piper and Justin Taylor (Wheaton: Crossway Books, 2007), 104.

[57] R. C. Sproul, The *Consequences of Ideas, Understanding the Concepts that Shaped our World*, (Crossway Books, 2000), 93. Gottfried Wilhelm Leibniz, born in 1646, an accomplished mathematician was credited as creating the theory of *pre-established harmony*. "Each individual unit of reality, or (monad), acts according to its peculiar, created purpose. Though each monad exist in virtual isolation from every other monad, monads act together in symphonic harmony (community)."

[58] Brian McLaren, *A New Kind of Christian. A Tale of Two Friends on a Spiritual Journey* (San Francisco: Jossey-Bass, 2001), 101.

[59] Ibid.

[60] Michael J. Kruger, "The Sufficiency of Scripture in Apologetics," http://www.tms.edu/tmsj/tmsj12m.pdf

[61] Paul Wells, "The Doctrine of Scripture: Only a Human Problem" in *Reforming or Conforming. Post-Conservative Evangelicals and the Emergent Church*, eds. Gary L. W. Johnson and Ronald N. Gleason (Wheaton: Crossway Books, 2008), 31.

[62] Ibid.

[63] http://www.baylor.edu/content/services/document.php/87233.pdf

[64] Semiologist- a proponent of semiology which is the study of signs and its operation in a given system. Language, mass media and even fashion are areas considered for study by semiology.

[65] Stuart Sims and Borin Van Boon, *Introduction to Critical theory, A Graphic Guide* (London: Icon Books, 2009), 72.

[66] Martin Downes, "Entrapment" in *Reforming or Conforming? Post-Conservative Evangelicals and the Emergent Church* eds. Gary L. W. Johnson and Ronald N. Gleason (Wheaton: Crossway Books, 2008), 238-239.

[67] *The Timeless Writings of C.S. Lewis* (New York: Inspirational Press, 1981), 361-362.

[68] David F. Wells, *The Courage to be Protestant* (Grand Rapids: Eerdsmans Publishing Co., 2008), 15-17.

[69] Ronald H. Preston, *Confusions in Christian Social Ethics*, (London: SCM Press Ltd., 1994), 6.

[70] Postmodern deconstruction – a concept brought into vogue by Jacques Derrida a proponent of post-structionalism which focuses on the meaning in a text versus meaning perceived by the reader of the text. Deconstruction is a method that seeks to analyze all forms of human communication to the extent of breaking it down to the most subtle components of inconsistencies, thusly undermining itself.

[71] Paul Wells, "The Doctrine of Scripture: Only a Human Problem" in *Reforming or Conforming. Post-Conservative Evangelicals and the Emerging Church*. eds. Gary L.W. Johnson and Ronald N. Gleason (Wheaton: Crossway books, 2008), 30 (emphasis added).

[72] Doug Pagitt, *Reimagining Spiritual Formation: A Week in the Life of an Experimental Church* (Grand Rapids: Zondervan, 2004), 4-5.

[73] Ronald N. Gleason "Church and Community or Community and Church?"in *Reforming or Conforming? Post-Conservative Evangelicals and the Emerging Church* eds. Gary L.W. Johnson and Ronald N. Gleason (Wheaton: Crossway Books, 2008), 176.

[74] Ibid.

[75] Brian McLaren, *New Kind of Christian*, (San Francisco: Jossey Bass, 2001), 158.

[76] Joel B. Green and Mark D. Baker, *Recovering the Scandal of the Cross* (Downers Grove: InterVarsity Press, 2000), 30.

[77] Brian McLaren, *Generous Orthodoxy* (Grand Rapids: Zondervan, 2004), 223.

[78] John Piper and Justin Taylor eds., *The Supremacy of Christ in the Postmodern World* (Wheaton: Crossway Books, 2007).

[79] Mark Driscoll, Confessions of a Reformission Rev.: Hard Lessons from an Emerging Missional Church (Grand Rapids: Zondervan, 2006), 150.

[80] Biblical Discernment Ministries, "Robert Schuller. General Teachings/Activites," http://www.rapidnet.com/~jbeard/ bdm/exposes/schuller/general.htm

[81] "Sin is any failure to conform to the moral law of God in act, attitude, or nature." Wayne Grudem, *Systematic Theology* (Grand Rapids: Zondervan, 1994), 490.

[82] Dr. R. A. Torrey- (1856-1928) was an American evangelist, pastor and educator who travelled the world in as an evangelistic endeavor and wrote extensively.

[83] Robert E. Webber, *Ancient-Future Faith. Rethinking Evangelicalism for a Postmodern World* (Grand Rapids: Baker Books, 1999).

[84] T. A. Mahon, "Ancient-Future Heresies," www.theberean-call.org/node/6535

[85] Robert Webber, *Listening in the Beliefs of Emerging Churches* (Grand Rapids: Zondervan, 2007), 199.

[86] Billy Graham Center, "The Chicago Call-Collection 33," www.wheaton.edu/bgc/archives/GUIDES/033.htm

[87] Chris Armstrong, "The Future Lies in the Past," www.christianity today.com/ct/2008/february/22.22/html

Mystical devotion-devotion that is based on intuition, meditative thoughts or conduct, that is, anything outside the realm of comprehension by human reasoning. In LT mystical devotion is based on the practices of Roman Catholic Desert Fathers and Eastern Orthodox.

[88] Chris Armstrong, "The Future Lies in the Past," www.Christianity Today.com/ct/2008/February/22.22.html

[89] Ibid.

[90] R. Kent Hughes, *Acts. The Church Afire* (Wheaton: Crossway Books, 1996), 68.

[91] Ibid., 13.

[92] R. Kent Hughes, *Acts. The Church Afire* (Wheaton: Crossway Books, 1996), 13.

[93] C. S. Lewis, *God in the Duck: Essays on Theology and Ethics* ed. Walter Hooper (Grand Rapids: Eerdsman, 1970), 95.

[94] Paul Wells, "The Doctrine of Scripture: Only a Human Problem" in *Reforming or Conforming? Post-Conservative Evangelicals and the Emerging Church.* eds. Gary L.W. Johnson and Ronald N. Gleason (Wheaton: Crossway Books, 2008), 43.

[95] Arnold B. Poole, The Orchard of the Holy Spirit, (Plymouth, Michigan: Colwell Publishers, 1977) 107.

[96] Josh McDowell and Bob Hostetler, Right From Wrong (Nashville: Thomas Nelson, 1994), 93.

[97] An editorial from the Washington Times, September, 28, 2009 entitled, "'Safe School' Czar Ignored Statutory Rape,"

http://www.sweetness-light.com/archive/safe-school-czar-ignored-statutory-rape

[98] Gary L. W. Johnson, "Introduction" in *Reforming or Conforming? Post-Conservative Evangelicals and the Emerging Church* eds. Gary L. W. Johnson and Ronald N. Gleason (Wheaton: Crossway Books, 2008), 16.

[99] Craig S. Carter, *Rethinking Christ and Culture. A Post-Christiandom Perspective* (Grand Rapids: Brazoo Press, 2006), 23.

[100] Dave Hunt, *Countdown to the Second Coming*, The Berean Call, Bend, OR, 2005.

[101] E. G. White, *America in Prophecy,* Jemison: Inspiration Books East, Inc., 1988.

[102] www.wikipedia.org/wik/JohnWycliffe

[103] Joan Wimmel Brown, ed., *The Martyred Christian,* New York, NY: Macmillian, 1985, 157.

About the Authors

Maria Brusco Osso and Deanna Blackmon Jones are currently doctoral candidates of Biblical Studies at Calvary Christian College and Graduate School in Waldorf, Maryland. Mrs. Jones is also the author of the book *The Faith Arena*.